SHAKESPEARE
AND THE
ROSE OF LOVE

SHAKESPEARE
and the
Rose of Love

A STUDY OF THE
EARLY PLAYS IN RELATION TO
THE MEDIEVAL PHILOSOPHY
OF LOVE

by

JOHN VYVYAN

1968
CHATTO & WINDUS
LONDON

Published by
Chatto & Windus Ltd
40-42 William IV Street
London W.C.2

*

Clarke, Irwin & Co. Ltd
Toronto

First Printed 1960
Reprinted 1968

SBN 7011 1175 5

© John Vyvyan 1960

Printed in Great Britain by
William Lewis (Printers) Ltd Cardiff

CONTENTS

For nothing this wide universe I call,
Save thou, my rose; in it thou art my all.

Is mihi "Lascivi" dixit "praeceptor Amoris,
duc, age, discipulos ad mea templa tuos,
est ubi diversum fama celebrata per orbem
littera, cognosci quae sibi quemque iubet.
qui sibi notus erit, solus sapienter amabit
atque opus ad vires exiget omne suas."

"Come, thou preceptor of light love, and
lead thy pupils to my temple. Thereon, is
an inscription famed throughout the earth
that commands each to know himself. Only
he who knows himself will love with wisdom,
and according to his powers, perform love's
work in full."

OVID

Chapter I

THE TERENTIAN PATTERN

IN 1584, at the age of twenty, Shakespeare left Stratford—a fugitive, perhaps, from the heavy-handed justice of Sir Thomas Lucy. What became of him for the next few years is unknown. As his earliest work cannot be dated with certainty, the length of this interval is not agreed upon. But by 1592 he had already made his mark in the London theatre—"an upstart crow", in the malicious words of poor Greene, "that is in his own conceit the only Shake-scene in a country". So however Shakespeare had spent the missing years, they would seem to have been conducive to his self-assurance.

Almost everything that a young Elizabethan might have done has been imagined of him in those eight years. In an age when brilliant panache was esteemed a virtue, it is likely that he did his best to give them colour; and one of the striking things about the early plays is the social accomplishment they imply in their author. From the first, he writes of high circles as if he felt at home in them, with confidence and fluency. In *Love's Labour's Lost*, he treats of the trivialities that are much harder to counterfeit than the formalities of society; and it does not appear that he ever blunders. That part of his *Wanderjahre* were spent, therefore, in a nobleman's household—where patronage may have ripened into friendship—seems to be a reasonable guess. But we do not know.

There is one fact, however, that I should like to stress: the earliest work that is certainly Shakespeare's is that of an experienced man. Twenty-eight is a late beginning for genius; many poets have reached their apogee by then. At that age, Keats was already dead, and Shelley had only two more years to live. Therefore, although the plays of Shakespeare's first period show that he had an immense amount to learn in the art of expressing his ideas, we should not be surprised that their thought-content is mature.

In boyhood, it is usually assumed, he went to Stratford Grammar School. If he did, he would have received an excellent literary education there. The Elizabethan grammar school was guided by the enlightened spirit of Erasmus. On the basis of the old trivium—grammar, rhetoric and logic—the Latin classics were conscientiously taught, and, in the higher forms, the Greek. Compared with a modern curriculum, the subjects were few; and for that reason, a much higher standard was obtained in them. But there are only two points about Shakespeare's early reading on which I should like to lay emphasis: he had been thoroughly grounded, as every Elizabethan schoolboy was, in the plays of Terence; and at some time, probably for his own delight, he had read Chaucer's translation, *The Romaunt of the Rose*. From Terence, and his commentators, he learnt the five-part construction of a play; and from *The Romaunt of the Rose* he learnt, among other things, the elements of the medieval philosophy of love.

> *Ce est li Romanz de la Rose*
> *Ou l'Art d'Amors est toute enclose.*

As the poem turned out, that is an over-statement. It does not embrace the whole art of love: both Dante and the Renaissance Neo-Platonists had much to add. But before we consider Shakespeare's debt to *The Romaunt of the Rose* we must look rather more briefly at what he owed to Terence.

*　　*　　*

The fact that Shakespeare and his contemporaries conceived their plays in five logical parts—although these were not necessarily presented as separate units on the stage—does not at first seem relevant to the theme of love. But I think it will be granted that structure may be a guide to meaning: and I hope to show that, in the present case, it is an important one. I have discussed elsewhere the temptation-sequence in Shakespeare.[1] This was incorporated later, its origins are different, and it need not detain us here.

The five-act structure, as the Renaissance understood it, was mainly derived from Roman comedy, and particularly from long study of the plays of Terence. I do not propose to analyse it in detail, but only in so far as it may give a clue to ideas in Shakespeare which we might otherwise miss. Essentially, it is a method of plot-construction, not of stage-presentation. We may consider the five acts as five phases of the story; but when an interval was needed in the theatre, it was natural to place it at the close of such a phase. The logic of this construction—although its first use was for light entertainment—will be readily revealed by a metaphor of war.

[1] *The Shakespearean Ethic*, p. 13 *et seq.*

Act I

We find that a war is about to break out. We are told the cause of it; the objective of each side is made clear to us; and our sympathies are definitely enlisted on one side only. Briefly, the first act gives the rational and emotional background of the coming action.

Act II

The action opens with the preliminary skirmishes and manœuvres of both armies. The main battle is not joined; but all the moves leading up to it are made, and we await it in suspense.

Act III

The battle begins with the attack of the side we hope will lose; but at the end of the act, it seems as if it is going to win. Our suspense is accordingly greater.

Act IV

The counter-attack is launched; and the act closes with everything prepared for the final victory, but just short of it.

Act V

There may be a *persona ex machina*, or twist of surprise. And then the crowning success of the side we always hoped would win.

There is sound dramatic logic in this. The opening satisfies the wish of the audience to be "in the know", gives it an outcome to hope for, and engages its sympathies. The action provides the conflict, which is the heart-beat of drama. The climatic point of each act creates mounting suspense. And the conclusion gives the audience its heart's desire. It is particularly suited to comedy, for which, of course, it was created; but it has been brilliantly adapted to other purposes. Reduced to schematic simplicity (with apologies to *The Lady of Andros*), Terence builds a plot on it somewhat as follows.

Act I

A young man is in love with a charming girl of whom his father disapproves, and he has promised to marry her. The father is determined that he shall marry someone else. Each of them is well-intentioned. Although no action has begun, it is clear that conflict lies ahead. The background of it is understood, the aim of each side is clear, and the sympathies of the audience are enlisted for the son.

Act II

The son finds that a friend of his is in love with the girl he does *not* want to marry; so, naturally, they join forces. There is also a clever slave—a little too clever, and by him an amusing knot of error is tied.

Act III

The father takes the field. He approaches the family of the girl he wants his son to marry, and wins their consent to the match. The wedding is to take place at once. The outlook is calamitous.

Act IV

The son and his allies make a counter-attack. This

is to let the family find out that he and his true-love have already had a baby. The wedding is therefore called off, and the situation is reversed.

Act V

Harmony is now to be established. It is discovered that the son's sweetheart is really a long-lost daughter of the other girl's family—in fact, the girls are sisters. The father withdraws his opposition, and finds that his son's own choice will be the perfect daughter-in-law after all. The second girl is paired with her right young man, and everyone is happy. There are no losers.

It will be seen that however nugatory the story may be, this construction gives it logic, balance and proportion. It is shaped consciously as a work of art. Without losing the artistic unity, a sub-plot can be interwoven, if required, to make the pattern as complex, yet well-designed as a cobweb. And this web may catch and exhibit the fleeting things of life, whether blue-bottles or dewdrops. In the knot-of-error kind of play, the opposing sides may represent error and truth, which can be taken as lightly or seriously as the author pleases. The audience naturally hopes that truth will prevail, and the interplay or conflict between them may be shaped according to the formula. This opens the way for an allegorical under-meaning; and so, no doubt, endeared the plan to Shakespeare. In general, the structure comes so logically to an entertaining story that many authors have used it, or approximated to it, without giving Terence a thought.

Later commentators reduced this construction to

three parts, which they termed protasis, epitasis and catastrophy. There was some difference of opinion as to where the protasis should end, and medieval commentaries confine it to the first act; but in the form in which the theory probably reached Shakespeare, it covered the first two. Baldwin has shown that there are good grounds for believing that the edition of Terence published by Willichius about 1550, with a preface by Wagnerus, in which he analyses the structure of the *Andria*, greatly influenced Shakespeare. Wagnerus, in the preface, distinguishes two internal goals for a play:

> The first goal is the thing towards which the protasis tends, at the end of the second act. The second is the thing towards which the epitasis tends, the occasion of the catastrophe, at the end of the fourth act. So the first and second acts form a sub-unit, as do the third and fourth. This integrated formula of Wagnerus (Willichius) gives a very definite framework indeed for constructing a play.[1]

On this analysis, then, the protasis is the content of the first two acts; that is, everything up to the decisive struggle. The epitasis is the third and fourth acts; that is, the whole decisive engagement, attack and counter-attack. And the catastrophe is the happy ending. The triple division is of less importance than the five-fold one, which became the norm of staging as well as of construction; but it is sometimes convenient, and when used in this book the definitions of Wagnerus will be assumed.

[1] Baldwin, *William Shakspere's Five-Act Structure,* p. 239. University of Illinois Press, 1947.

It is worth while to stress that these principles of construction were not a matter of recondite knowledge in the sixteenth century. Every grammar-school boy knew them. At the beginning of a new term at Winchester, in 1565, the headmaster included the following in his speech to the boys:

> Of comedies three parts are enumerated, pro-thesis, epitasis, catastrophe. But comedies are said to be imitations of those things which are in life, as there is no one who doubts that these same parts are in life. You know that there are also three stages in diseases, augmentation, state, decline. The same thing has happened to these holidays, for they have had a beginning, a middle, and an end—[1]

The importance of this pattern in Shakespeare is far greater than is usually assumed. He learnt the Terentian construction at the beginning of his career, and he was still using it in his maturity. It will give us a better sense of direction if we establish this end-point first, although it will necessitate a digression. If we date Shakespeare's earliest plays about 1590, we may look ahead twenty years to *The Winter's Tale* and find the Terentian formula clearly discernible.

Structurally, *The Winter's Tale* is perhaps the most fascinating of all Shakespeare's plays. I have pointed out elsewhere[2] that it exhibits the tragic sequence up to the end of the third act. Then there is a turning-point, marked by the confrontation with death. And the regeneration sequence leads up to the triumph of

---

[1] Baldwin: *William Shakspere's Small Latine and Lesse Greeke.* University of Illinois Press, 1944; vol. 1, p. 333.
[2] *The Shakespearean Ethic,* chapter 11.

love at the end. How these two elaborate patterns—and much else—are exactly fitted into a Terentian fabric is a constructional *tour de force*; but it is only the act-plotting that concerns us now.

Act I

The opposing forces are jealousy and love. Leontes represents jealousy, Hermione love. We are shown how jealousy was unreasonably awakened. We see the death-directed intrigue that jealousy sets afoot, the objective being Hermione's execution. And we see the counter-forces tending to reconciliation. Thus we have what Terence requires: the rational and emotional background of the conflict, clear objectives, and awakened sympathy.

Act II

There are preliminary moves by both sides. Those made by jealousy result in Hermione being sent to prison. Those made by love result in the new-born child being sent to Leontes, as an ambassadress of love. He rejects her. This concludes what the commentators call the protasis, everything leading up to the decisive struggle.

Act III

Jealousy—the side to which our sympathies are opposed—now launches its main offensive. Hermione is brought to trial, and all but condemned. We reach the blackest hour: the death of Leontes' son, the feigned death of Hermione, and the casting away of Perdita.

Act IV

This is the counter-action of love. The fourth act, as I have tried to show, is an allegory of the healing of the tragic wound by love. It also does everything that the Terentian rules require: it ends the epitasis, by providing the conditions for the final victory, and yet stops short of it.

Act V

Harmony is established. There are no losers, in spite of the preceding conflict. The unions of love form a perfect end.

The Winter's Tale has often been judged to be a poorly constructed play. But when we understand the principles on which Shakespeare planned it, we find it to be a miracle of construction. The ingenious use of the Terentian pattern is the least astonishing element in its design. Within this, Shakespeare has incorporated his hellward sequence and heavenward sequence, illustrated these with allegory, and made implicit a philosophy of life. But I must not digress into these complexities here; and if my readers will endure one more skeleton plot, we shall have taken our bearings, from this glance at Shakespeare's mature work, and return to the opening of his career. Another play in which tragedy is resolved, *Measure for Measure*, written in 1604, will also yield to a Terentian analysis.

Act I

The background plan of the Duke of Vienna is introduced, but not elucidated fully. Then we are given a clear-cut issue. Is Claudio to live or die? Angelo has sentenced him to death. Lucio and Isabella are trying to save him. Again, reduced to stark simplicity, there are death-directed forces, and life-directed forces. Conflict is immanent, and our sympathies are engaged on the side of life.

Act II

The usual preliminary moves and counter-moves take place; Lucio and Isabella intercede, the outcome is uncertain; Angelo counters with an unacceptable proposal. Claudio's chances seem definitely less. But the Duke's forces have not been committed to the battle yet, and we do not doubt that they will be. So the protasis ends here.

Act III

The death-forces play their trump card, which is to win over Isabella. Now she also condemns Claudio, "Die, perish!" His case looks hopeless, and he gives it up himself. But the Duke begins to pull the strings.

Act IV

The life-forces, now directed by the Duke, play their trump card, which is to bring in Mariana. She represents the active power of love. We are left convinced that they will win, but uncertain how. This ends the epitasis.

Act V

The "power divine" of the Duke, supported by the love-power of Mariana pleading for life, accomplish much more than the saving of Claudio: there is an all-inclusive victory for love and life.

We may now see that, especially in the plays of resolution of tragedy, it would be difficult to over-estimate the importance of the Terentian influence—difficult, but not impossible; because there is so much more in them besides. In analysis, these plays all show a life-intrigue and a death-intrigue in conflict. The death-powers and their activities are more complex; but of the life-powers we are now in a position to establish some important constants. Life always plays its trump card in the fourth act; and it is usually the same card—love. This is exhibited dramatically by the activity and fortunes of the character who is, in her second nature, the allegorical figure either of love itself or of the beauty by which love is awakened.

Portia's intervention turns the scale in the fourth act of *The Merchant of Venice*, although Shylock had seemed to be triumphant in the third. Mariana enters in the fourth act of *Measure for Measure*, and her pleading for life in the fifth is decisive. The fourth act of *The Winter's Tale* belongs to Perdita, who is Hermione's second self. And although *The Tempest* is not spun so exactly as a Terentian web, its fourth act is the "marriage" of Miranda and Ferdinand, whence a new world of concord will spring. Conversely, when love is murdered, as it was by Othello, or rejected, as by Hamlet, the hero's destruction is inevitable. This establishes the primary significance of the allegorical figure of Love, whatever her name may be, beyond equivocation: she is the trump card of life; and if the life-forces play this card, and still lose the trick, then the outcome is certain death.

In any romantic story, of course, love-interest

centres on the heroine; but in these plays she has an allegorical importance as well. Her fortunes, in the epitasis of all of them, determine the outcome of life or death. She is a love-symbol. And the love-symbol, for Shakespeare, is something more than sex, passion or romance; these are parts, but their sum is not the whole. If we could discover the full significance that this figure had for Shakespeare, it would illuminate nearly all his work; because very few plays are without it. So it seems worth while to try to lift a corner of the curtain, and I propose to make this our main enquiry. Inevitably, there will be asides. Shakespeare did not invent the philosophy of love, although he shaped his borrowings into his own design; and we shall have to delve into the minds of some of his precursors.

It should, perhaps, be stressed that to lift a corner of the curtain is all that this book aims to do. Shakespeare is drawing on three traditions in this connection: courtly love, with the mystical associations that gathered round the Rose; Platonic love, as the Renaissance understood and in a measure created it; and the redemptive love of the Gospels. To assess his debt to the first of these is my present endeavour. I hope this will clear the way to a fuller understanding of the influence on him of the other two. But Shakespeare's Platonism, in particular, is too large a subject to be treated as an adjunct to any other; and I will therefore defer consideration of the content of Platonic beauty in his heroines. But since his view of love and beauty was, I think, that they are the dynamic and static aspects of one reality, there is no contradiction in his using the same figure to represent them.

21

By-paths have to be explored; but as they are some-times bewildering, I should like, even at the risk of seeming repetitive, to make clear the direction of the highway. I will therefore state a general proposition first. In one sense, the heroine is mainly passive, a "transparent Helena", in and through whom, if all goes well, the hero discovers the celestial beauty; and the background philosophy of this is principally renaissance Neo-Platonism. In another and more dramatic sense, she is active, and then she displays the creative and redemptive power of love. These aspects cannot be separated completely, but the second will be our chief concern.

Chapter II

"LOVE'S LABOUR'S LOST"

IT is fortunately not necessary to our present enquiry to go into the vexed question of whether *Love's Labour's Lost* is Shakespeare's first extant play. Traditionally, it has long been considered so—and dated about 1590; but among contemporary critics, there is a sharp conflict of opinion. The title-page of the first Quarto describes it as "Newly corrected and augmented". It is clear that it has been augmented. There must, then, have been two versions. We may assume that the first of these was, at least, a very early work, and that important additions were made to it—possibly some years later. The augmentations show an evolution of thought, which is not the product of mere polishing, but of time. And so the tradition that places the first version—but not the full text we now possess—at the head of the list, may well be sound. Chronological certainty is not possible. But from the point of view of Shakespeare's exploration of love, this may be taken as the beginning—"*Incipit Vita Nova*".

The act-structure has suffered in consequence of the alterations. In the text we now have, there is great disproportion between the acts—the first having less than two hundred lines, and the last, nine hundred and forty. There may have been cuts as well as additions to the original. In spite of this, the Terentian plan is well marked. Naturally, the design was made for the simpler, earlier version; and it cannot be expected to display the deeper philosophy that was afterwards put in. It does a little to illuminate the play's more significant ideas, and we will therefore present it briefly.

Act I

We find that the dramatic conflict of the comedy is to be between learning and love. The real battleground is, therefore, in the hearts, or minds, of the characters. And our sympathies are enlisted for love.

Act II

Learning makes a defensive move: the ladies are forbidden to enter the court. Love makes a countermove: though shut out from the house, the ladies slip into the gentlemen's hearts. This ends the protasis.

Act III

A knot of error is tied: the clown is entrusted with the love-letters of the lords, which he later delivers to the wrong ladies.

Act IV

The tide turns in favour of love: the young men discover each other's attachments, and Berowne proves to them that all true learning begins with love. This ends the epitasis.

Act V

After some vicissitudes, the lovers are accepted by their ladies; but a preliminary penance is imposed on each. These penances are, in fact, a deeper sort of learning; so neither side has really lost. Some shallow notions, both of learning and of love, have been dismissed; and the profundities of each are shown as one.

Much more, it may be noticed, is implicit in this conclusion than we expect from a comedy; but Shakespeare is certainly employing the Terentian plan. He has not yet learnt to do so very deftly, and his subsequent alterations have put it sadly out of shape; but even so, it affords some clues which we must try to follow.

*   *   *

In this play, we find a number of young people on the threshold of life, and the question it poses could not be more appropriate. What is the aim of life? The question is framed, What is the end of study? But it is the deeper problem that Shakespeare is putting both to himself and to his audience.

The characters we meet first are the young King of Navarre, and three of his lords—the *jeunesse dorée* of a Renaissance court; but the atmosphere is a blend of serious thinking and spirited fooling with which universities are familiar, and the audience easily participates in the emotional situation. Most of us have thought, at some time, that we should like to be famous, and that if we studied hard enough we might succeed; and most of us have had second thoughts, that it would be much more fun to dress up as Russians and tease the girls; and probably we have had third thoughts, that real love demands real sacrifices and that to make them is well worth while. The King of Navarre passes through these not unusual phases; and so, we may suppose, had Shakespeare; but on this familiar topic he has something out of the ordinary to say.

He does not say it, in full, until the last scene; and then it is more than we expect. Until near the end, the play had seemed to be a comedy. Abruptly we discover it is not:

> Our wooing doth not end like an old play;
> Jack hath not Jill: these ladies' courtesy
> Might well have made our sport a comedy.   V. ii

If it is not a comedy, what is it? "Tragedy, history, pastoral, pastoral-comical . . . ?" But Polonius is mocking definitions, without providing the right one. And it may be that our usual terminology is inappropriate to Shakespearean drama; for if it leads us to assume standards with which Shakespeare was not attempting to comply, it will cause confusion. Perhaps our knowledge of his full aims is still inadequate to determine how far he fell short, as every artist must, of attaining them. But we will not pursue these questions yet. With regard to the present play, Shakespeare has simply told us that it might have been a comedy, but it is not; and we may class it provisionally as a play with a "message".

The message turns out to be Shakespeare's answer—not, of course, his final answer, but the one he had reached in sincerity as a young man—to a double question: What is the aim of life, and how is it to be attained? Whether the answer is important in itself is a matter of opinion; but since Shakespeare thought it was, it is important to an understanding of his future work: it is a foundation.

26

His way of persuading us that the aim he finally proposes is the right one, is to set up a number of others—plausible but inadequate—and to laugh these off the stage: what remains when we have ceased laughing, and we do cease laughing in the last act, is, in his view, the truth. As this is a method of weeding the brain which he uses elsewhere, it is worth notice. In this play, the hint is given to us by the Princess of France, when she says to her ladies:

We are wise girls to mock our lovers so.   V. ii

This is what Shakespeare is also doing to these characters—mocking them, but not unkindly. In intention, it is a wise mockery, with the purpose of removing their imperfections and leaving them true men. And he is particular, in several places, to distinguish it from sarcasm and scorn. Rosaline, for instance, says to Berowne:

                    —the world's large tongue
Proclaims you for a man replete with mocks,
Full of comparisons and wounding flouts,
Which you on all estates will execute
That lie within the mercy of your wit.

This habit, she tells him, is wormwood, which he must weed from his character before she will accept him:

A jest's prosperity lies in the ear
Of him that hears it, never in the tongue
Of him that makes it—   V. ii

So Shakespeare, I suggest, has defined for us the principle he is now following: he makes fun of the affectations of these characters, so that they may be rid of them and discover themselves. He gets a great deal

27

of enjoyment from their foibles; but even to the most preposterous of them—Armado, Nathaniel and Holofernes—in spite of their absurdities, he is not unkind. A number of fine-seeming but unfruitful ideas are being put to the test of life and laughter.

* * *

In the opening scene, the aim of life that the king proposes to the three young lords is to be famous when they are dead:

> Let fame, that all hunt after in their lives,
> Live register'd upon our brazen tombs,
> And then grace us in the disgrace of death— I. i

This immortality in brass is to be won by study; and like all great victories it will be costly. The programme for the pursuit of fame that the king has drawn up, and in which the others have promised to keep him company, requires, in effect, the sacrifice of present life and all its disturbing emotions. They are to spend three years in monastic devotion to learning. During that time they will have one meal a day and fast altogether one day a week, they will sleep only three hours each night and not doze in between, and they will see no ladies—indeed, no woman is to be allowed within a mile of the court on penalty of losing her tongue. This is more than a plan, it is a command performance; and so the king exhorts them:

> Therefore, brave conquerors—for so you are,
> That war against your own affections
> And the huge army of the world's desires—
> Our late edict shall strongly stand in force:
> Navarre shall be the wonder of the world— I. i

The edict is reinforced by a document, setting out these forbidding rules, which each of them is to sign:

> You three, Berowne, Dumain, and Longaville,
> Have sworn for three years' term to live with me,
> My fellow-scholars, and to keep those statutes
> That are recorded in this schedule here:
> Your oaths are pass'd; and now subscribe your names,
> That his own hand may strike his honour down
> That violates the smallest branch herein—   I. i

Dumain and Longaville sign submissively. Berowne also signs, but it is his part to protest. The king's goal lies in the future, so far off that it is beyond the horizon of mortality: Berowne therefore—on the assumption that "the future was invented to spoil the present"— puts the case for living now:

> At Christmas I no more desire a rose
> Than wish a snow in May's new-fangled shows,
> But like each thing that in its season grows.   I. i

The season of this play, in every sense, is spring: it is the month of May. And so Berowne is naturally putting the case for love, "whose month is ever May". The audience is led to feel that this point of view is right: the king, with his concern for autumn fruit, is trying to live at the wrong time of year. But Berowne is not opposed to learning, provided that the subject be well-chosen:

> Study me how to please the eye indeed,
> By fixing it upon a fairer eye—

To do this, he suggests, will illuminate the student,

instead of damaging his sight. It will be pleasanter
and more valuable, since little is to be won from words:

> These earthly godfathers of heaven's lights,
>   That give a name to every fixed star,
> Have no more profit of their shining nights
>   Than those that walk and wot not what they
>   are.
> Too much to know is to know naught but fame;
> And every godfather can give a name.   I. i

In view of what is to come, we may notice that
Shakespeare implies more by these lines than the
meaning that suffices in this context. The name is not
the star, the word is not the truth. And it is to the real
nature of the star—love, in this play—that he will
lead his characters at last. Meanwhile, Berowne has
put the case for living in season, and enlisted the
sympathies of the audience, although the king's
rejoinder is undeniably apt:

> How well he's read, to reason against reading!
>   I. i

Although they all laugh at him, Berowne is not
silenced; he carries the argument deeper: this studious
seclusion, to which they are now in honour vowed, is a
dereliction of duty. This is his best card, with which
he will take the act. He has already predicted that
natural temptations will make them all foresworn; now
he reminds the king that the oath, if kept to the letter,
will conflict with his obligations. For reasons of state,
he must receive the Princess of France, who is coming
on a special embassy from her father. Berowne thus
exposes the vow as a monstrosity:

So study evermore is over-shot;
While it doth study to have what it would,
It doth forget to do the thing it should—   I. i

And the thing it should is not the pursuit of fame, recorded on a brazen tomb, but first of all the discharge of human responsibilities and the exploration of the possibilities of life. The king admits that he had forgotten the princess, and will have to meet her; and henceforth the oath is merely a joke—the question is not whether it will be broken, but when and how. It is altogether shattered, in the end; and yet learning itself is not discredited, but only the kind of learning that is divorced from loving and living. And we are left with the impression that these things should not be frag-ments, but a whole: each has need of the others.

Since temptations become immensely important in Shakespeare's mature work, it is interesting to see that even at this stage he has begun to take notice of their dramatic possibilities; but, which is surprising, the first use he makes of them is for laughter. The young men have taken an oath which they ought not to have taken; and so, when they are tempted to break it, they are really being "tempted" to do right. This is ingenious and amusing; and it alerts us to a more important point: Shakespeare's structural principles remain remarkably similar whatever kind of play he is writing. And as his work proceeds, we begin to suspect that he is aiming to create an ideal dramatic form— founded on Terence, but vastly enriched—that will suit all the purposes Polonius could think of, or even that Shakespeare himself had in mind.

*   *   *

31

Postponing consideration of the sub-plot, we may now pass to the second act. The Princess of France and her retinue, including three provocative ladies—one for each of the king's lords we rightly guess—have arrived. But her gentleman-in-waiting, Boyet, informs her:

> Navarre had notice of your fair approach—
>   —Marry, thus much I have learnt:
> He rather means to lodge you in the field,
> Like one that comes here to besiege his court,
> Than seek a dispensation for his oath—   II. i

In this, there is a clear ring of challenge; for she is not only a brilliantly witty princess, but also, we must certainly infer, the allegorical figure of Love and Beauty; and it is presumptuous for a young man, king though he be, to keep her waiting in the fields.

The king is still resolved to keep his oath to study. In point of fact, his true education is about to begin, but not in the way he has planned; nor is it in the way we expect, if we are thinking of an *éducation sentimentale*. The king is to be instructed in love; but we must beware of putting a present-day construction on that word. Shakespeare is thinking of it, in this context, as many poets of the Middle Ages did—that is, religiously. This is not at once apparent; but it becomes so, when the penances are imposed at the end of the play.

We are being led, here, to the conclusion that learning without love is pedantry; and this may be a first step towards the much greater affirmation of later plays that justice without love is tyranny. In all Shakespeare's work, love is the star by which his characters must set their course; when they do not, their power and their learning only assist the storm that drives them to disaster. And however lightly Shakespeare seems to be writing, he is illustrating this philosophy.

The king and his lords now visit the princess and her ladies "in the field". His intention is to arrange a quick settlement of the affairs of Aquitaine, which was the purpose of the embassy, and to part; but while he and the princess are discussing business, the lords and ladies are falling for each other. Fortunately, the most important state-document is missing; and as no agreement can be reached without it, the princess must stay. She is to be kept, however, at what seems to be a safe distance; but when the king takes his leave, he makes a slip of the tongue which betrays to the audience how much he is endangered:

> You may not come, fair princess, in my gates;
> But here without you shall be so received
> As you shall deem yourself lodged in my heart,
> Though so denied fair harbour in my house—
> To-morrow shall we visit you again.   II. i

Though debarred from his court, the princess has slipped into his heart; and her ladies have been equally successful with his book-mates. The young men are now all in love. They are ashamed of being so, and are at great pains to hide the fact from one another. But theirs is still a very light kind of love—not nearly good enough for Shakespeare or his heroines. The men are looking down on this divine quality, and Shakespeare is determined that they—like all his characters, except those he has doomed—shall look up to it. They have now reached the stage of sighs and sonnets, which is

33

all very well for a while; but they are by no means
ready for the sacrifices that real love entails.

*   *   *

In the brief third act, Berowne is the first to give
himself away to the audience; but he commits the much
greater indiscretion of making Costard, the rustic
clown, his postman. He gives Costard a shilling, and a
letter to be delivered to one of the princess's ladies,
Rosaline:

> —ask for her,
> And to her white hand see thou do commend
> This seal'd-up counsel. III. i

Costard has another letter to deliver, and being unable
to read, he gives them to the wrong people, with the
consequence that Berowne's love-letter finds its way,
in the next act, to the king. This seal'd-up counsel
concludes with the couplet:

> Celestial as thou art, O, pardon love this wrong,
> That sings heaven's praise with such an earthly
>   tongue. IV. ii

An earthly tongue would have been pardonable
enough, but what is not to be excused is an insincere
one. Berowne does indeed suppose himself to be in
love; but his true opinion of Rosaline is that she is
anything but celestial; and he has no sooner dispatched
Costard with the letter, which purports to sing heaven's
praises, than he discloses his opinion to us, in a
soliloquy of the utmost candour:

> What! I love! I sue! I seek a wife!
> A woman, that is like a German clock,
> Still a-repairing, ever out of frame,
> And never going aright— III. i

34

Which is she, a celestial being or a German clock? We may form an opinion later; in the meantime, it is certain that Berowne is a hypocrite, and his love-letter a composition of vanity. But his education, like the king's, is in progress, and part of it is gradually to discover these unflattering facts. His next soliloquy shows some advance:

> Well, I do nothing in the world but lie, and lie in my throat. By heaven, I do love: and it hath taught me to rhyme, and to be melancholy. . . . Well, she hath one o' my sonnets already; the clown bore it, the fool sent it, and the lady hath it: sweet clown, sweeter fool, sweetest lady!   IV. iii

In fact, the lady has not got it; and it will shortly be returned by the clown to the fool, to prick the bubble of his deception; but before that happens, he will have the consolation of finding himself in good company.

The scene which follows is a parody of the ridiculous convention—one more inheritance from Roman comedy—of a number of characters being on stage together, and not merely failing to see one another, but declaiming their secrets aloud. Shakespeare himself was no realist in the theatre; he makes serious use of asides, soliloquies, allegory and more; but it is likely that he laughed at this convention of Terence, and here, in one of his moods of mockery, he shows it as preposterous.

The king enters, with a paper. Berowne steps behind a bush. The king heaves a sigh, and Berowne, delighted, murmurs, "Shot, by heaven! Proceed, sweet Cupid;—" The king does proceed, reading aloud a sonnet he has composed to the princess. Only a little less unearthly than Berowne's, it ends with the couplet:

> O queen of queens! how far dost thou excel,
> No thought can think, nor tongue of mortal tell.
>
> IV. iii

This he drops, in the simple hope that she will pick it up. Then he too hears a step, and hides behind a second bush. Longaville enters, with a paper, and the king whispers, "In love, I hope—" He is not disappointed. Longaville recites a sonnet he has written to Maria, in which he exonerates himself from oathbreaking on the grounds:

> A woman I forswore; but I will prove,
> Thou being a goddess, I forswore not thee;
> My vow was earthly, thou a heavenly love;
> Thy grace being gain'd cures all disgrace in me.
>
> IV. iii

Berowne mutters a sardonic aside:

> This is the liver-vein, which makes flesh a deity,
> A green goose a goddess: pure, pure idolatry.
>
> IV. iii

So now a green goose has joined the German clock. And Berowne is still "much out o' the way". Adding a sneer to an affectation has not brought him nearer to the truth; for there is a deity, we shall find, and it is through the earthly love that the heavenly will be discovered. Once more, a step is heard. Longaville hides; and the third lord, Dumain, enters moaning, "O, most divine Kate!" After this, they expose each other; but Berowne, the biggest humbug of them all, comes out last:

> Now step I forth to whip hypocrisy.　　IV. iii

There is no one, he supposes, who can show him up;
and so he flays his fellow-sinners without mercy:

> I am betray'd, by keeping company
> With men like you, men of inconstancy.
> When shall you see me write a thing in rhyme?
> Or groan for love? or spend a minute's time
> In pruning me? When shall you hear that I
> Will praise a hand, a foot, a face, an eye,
> A gait, a state, a brow, a breast, a waist,
> A leg, a limb? IV. iii

The contriving of such situations—where the
accuser is guilty of the offence for which he condemns
others—is one of Shakespeare's favourite devices,
which he never ceases to use. In comedy, we may call
it a trick. But when we find it in tragedy, employed
with deep seriousness, we must surely lift it to the
status of a principle. Berowne's own reference to the
"mote" and the "beam" shows that even here, in
Shakespeare's mind, it is related to deeper things; even
in this seemingly frivolous context, he is beginning to
ponder the nature of justice; and the problem, which is
inseparable from his enquiry into the nature of love,
becomes one of the great preoccupations of his maturity.
If the judge is morally no better than the person he
condemns, and often—as in *Measure for Measure* and
The Winter's Tale—worse, then where is justice? There
is no light answer to this question; and Shakespeare
wrestles with it in his major work, to come, as I think,
to a momentous conclusion. It would be astonishing
to find the beginnings of it—together with the
temptation theme, and other of his basic concepts
shortly to be displayed—in comedy, if we had not

37

already been alerted to the fact that he is seeking, among so many other things, an ideal dramatic structure adaptable to every need.

When Berowne has blown his bubble of censorious hypocrisy to its maximum, Costard the clown enters, with Jaquenetta. She is carrying the sonnet that should have been delivered to Rosaline, and she naïvely hands it to the king. He orders Berowne to read it aloud. Instead of doing so, Berowne tears it up:

> A toy, my liege, a toy: your Grace needs not fear it.
> LONGAVILLE: It did move him to passion, and there-fore let's hear it.
> DUMAIN (*gathering up the pieces*): It is Berowne's writing, and here is his name.
> BEROWNE (*to Costard*): Ah, you whoreson loggerhead! you were born to do me shame.—
> Guilty, my lord, guilty; I confess, I confess.

And then to them all:

> Sweet lords, sweet lovers, O, let us embrace!
> As true we are as flesh and blood can be:
> The sea will ebb and flow, heaven show his face;
> Young blood will not obey an old decree.
>
> IV. iii

It is not Berowne, but Shakespeare, who has whipped hypocrisy—but only with mirth. The lords are now agreed that their "guilt" is equal, and that none of them has the moral right to condemn another. Once again, a principle has been established in comedy which will be used in tragedy with tremendous power.

*   *   *

So far, the young men have discerned nothing but

the surface of love, and their ensuing conversation looks like a return to the "liver-vein"—pure, pure nonsense. Each maintains that his own mistress is "heavenly", but that no other qualifies for this distinction. Shakespeare may be mocking the common notion of lovers that their sweethearts are all divine exceptions; but possibly, for even in a light context an under-meaning is not to be ruled out, he may be seeing each of these ladies as a dual figure—as a woman of flesh and blood, and as a symbol. He does this so frequently in a serious way, that even here, I think, it is the correct explanation.

This idea of the duality of love—mortal form and eternal essence—is not, of course, his own. We might call it a convention, if that chilly word were not so inadequate for something deeply felt, of the medieval "religion" of love. Shakespeare owes much to this tradition, according to which the beloved is something more than herself: she has also a sacramental quality, partly revealing, partly veiling love's transcendence.

As this principle is important, we must briefly digress. I apologize for breaking off to explore tributary streams; but unless we do so, the main river of Shakespearean thought may remain as mysterious as the Nile before its sources had been mapped; and the dual nature of heroines is a contribution from the past. The idea is expressed in a variety of ways by medieval poets. Dante speaks of, "*La seconda bellezza che tu cele*", the second beauty that is concealed within you. Chrétien de Troyes shows his hero worshipping his mistress, in a way that can be understood only if we see that the act is conceived as a sacrament; otherwise it would be a blasphemy, which it certainly is not. And in *Roman de la Rose*, to Chaucer's translation of which Shakespeare was, I believe, indebted, the symbolic nature of this devotion is made clear by introducing the god of love as well as the lady. Even with these poets, of course, the idea is not original; but we cannot pursue an indefinite regression, and from our present point of view they may be treated as origins.

The Romaunt of the Rose appears to me to be a pervasive presence in Shakespeare's early love-plays. This Chaucerian version of part of the old French *Roman de la Rose* was first printed by William Thynne, in 1532, and it is likely that Shakespeare used that edition.[1] It is true that the ideas it presents could have reached him indirectly; but as Thynne's edition was available, it is a fair assumption that he found them there.

At the moment, I wish only to establish the relationship, in *The Romance of the Rose*, between the god of love, the lover and the lady. When the hero of the poem is pierced by the five arrows—that is to say, when he falls in love—it is not to the lady that he kneels. In fact he turns away from her, to the god of love who commands his service. From this moment, more than courtship is involved. Even if the lady were to die—as Dante's Beatrice did—the lover would still be a person dedicated to an ideal. Once smitten, he addresses the god as his liege lord:

> And I answered ful humbly
> Gladly sir / at your byddyng

[1] The Chaucer Society has issued a reprint of this edition. Chaucer Texts, First Series, LXXXII.

I wol me yelde in al thyng
To your seruyce I wol me take
For god defende that I shulde make
Ayen your byddyng resystence
I wol not don so great offence
For if I dyd / it were no skyll
Ye may do with me what ye wyll
Save or spyll /   1953

And if ye lyst of me to make
Your prisoner / I wol it take
Of herte and wyll fully at gre
Holy and playne I yelde me—   1970

He then kneels, and would have kissed the god's feet,
but he is prevented from doing this. He has made the
right answer; and therefore Love kisses him on the
mouth, telling him this is a special grace:

For curteys / and of fayre manere
Well taught / and ful of gentylnysse
He muste ben / that shal me kysse   2006

For I am of the selfe manere
Gentyll / curteys / meke / and fre—   2021

What, we may ask, has all this to do with falling in
love? Simply that the point of view of the Middle Ages
was a religious one. From the moment when the young
man in the poem becomes the lover, he embraces a new
way of life; and this will change his relationship to
everything. We tend to confine love to a concentration
of emotion—sometimes of devastating passion—on
an individual; but for the medieval lover this might be
only a beginning. The conclusion might be the *Divina
Commedia*, or some other diffusion of love's essence
through a wider sphere. It is therefore necessary to

recognize the god, or his equivalent, as well as the lady. And having done that, it is not illogical to regard love as a power which brings harmony to a discordant world. But the god is, of course, a convenient symbol for a principle—in Shakespeare's view, the sovereign principle—which ultimately resides in the self. So it need not surprise us that to be true to oneself and to be true to love become, in Shakespeare's usage, interchangeable expressions.

It may be thought inopportune to sound this deeper note at a moment when Shakespeare is entertaining us with light music. But I do so to emphasize a point: the dual nature of his heroines—and of some other characters as well—is not confined to the portentous plays, tragedies and resolutions of tragedy; it is safer, in fact, to look on it as an habitual element in his technique, and even in apparently unlikely places to bear it in mind. Richard David says of *Love's Labour's Lost* that, "beneath the shimmering surface the waters are deep".[1] And we may accordingly suspect the presence of those devices that Shakespeare uses to explore the deeps.

This suspicion is strengthened when we find that two, at least, of the men begin with a debased idea of love. In later plays, this becomes an infallible indication with Shakespeare that a man is on the wrong track— Hamlet, Angelo and Othello, for instance, blacken the women who love them, and this is a necessary step in their fall. The germ of this perversion is clearly present in *Love's Labour's Lost*, notably in the sub-plot. Armado says of Jaquenetta:

[1] *Love's Labour's Lost*, Arden edition, 1951; Introduction xvi.

I do affect the very ground, which is base, where
her shoe, which is baser, guided by her foot, which
is basest, doth tread. . . . Love is a familiar; Love is
a devil; there is no evil angel but Love.   I. ii

And Berowne says of Rosaline:

> And, among three, to love the worst of all;
> A whitely wanton with a velvet brow,
> With two pitch-balls stuck in her face for eyes;
> Ay, and, by heaven, one that will do the deed,
> Though Argus were her eunuch and her guard:
> And I do sigh for her! to watch for her!
> To pray for her! Go to; it is a plague—   III. i

But it is these base-seeming creatures who will re-
educate the scornful lords.

It may also be well to notice, parenthetically, that
what I have termed technique and device is by no
means wholly artificial; it has a correspondence with
psychological facts that seem to have been better
understood in the thirteenth century than in the nine-
teenth, although psycho-analysis is now beginning to
rediscover them. The object of love needs to be distinguished from love's power or cause, for they are
disproportionate; and a tradition which recognizes a
transcendence, conveniently symbolized as a god,
although many other symbols will serve, is in some
degree a safeguard against certain devastating emotional
states—such as that which poor Hazlitt records of himself in the *Liber Amoris*—which may occasionally
become suicidal or insane.

*   *   *

After the ludicrous dispute on the divinity of sweet-hearts, the king calls for calm:

> Then leave this chat; and, good Berowne, now prove
> Our loving lawful, and our faith not torn.
>
> IV. iii

Dumain also requests, "Some salve for perjury", and Berowne supplies it in his celebrated speech.

This is of particular interest from several points of view. In the first place it is really two speeches. The original ends at line 317,[1] and at some unknown later date, Shakespeare expanded it. What we now possess is two versions running consecutively. When Shakespeare refashions his earlier work in this manner, it is never for the sake of padding, but usually to present some new idea to which he has come to attribute special importance. By separating the two versions, we see immediately what the fresh conception is:

> But love, first learned in a lady's eyes,
> Lives not alone immured in the brain,
> But, with the motion of all elements,
> Courses as swift as thought in every power,
> And gives to every power a double power
> Above their functions and their offices.
>
> . . . . .
>
> Never durst poet touch a pen to write
> Until his ink were temper'd with love's sighs:
> O, then his lines would ravish savage ears,
> And plant in tyrants mild humility.
>
> . . . . .

---

[1] The line numbering is that of *The Oxford Shakespeare*; in the Arden Edition it is line 314.

It is religion to be thus forsworn;
For charity itself fulfils the law,
And who can sever love from charity?   IV. iii

These lines carry us far away from romantic comedy:
Shakespeare is saying that love is power. It is a power
that can quell tyranny, a power that in itself fulfils the
law. We cannot be sure that at this period he foresaw
the mighty employment to which he would put this
assertion; but it contains the principle by which, in his
culminating plays, he resolves tragedy, not simply by
arresting its course, but by transforming it into
regeneration. In *Measure for Measure*, for instance, it
is self-knowledge and love which transmute seeming
virtue into forth-going virtue, that is, into the power
by which, and by which alone, the deathward movement is brought to a stop, and an impulse towards life
is imparted.

To speak of love as power may be commonplace; but
to believe it is astonishing. In fact, one has to look to
the great religious figures—the Christ or the Buddha—
to find a consistent application of love to human affairs.
Neither Church nor State believes it to be practicable;
and both enforce their decrees by other means. Did
Shakespeare really have this faith? We can only say
that his plays proclaim it, and that he resolves tragedy
on that assumption. Whatever his personal belief may
have been, the proposition that love is power becomes
an important part of what we may call his "dramatic"
religion.

The inserting, at a later date, of this new conception
into Berowne's speech, shatters the logical continuity
of *Love's Labour's Lost*. If Berowne had really reached

45

this pinnacle by the end of the fourth act, then much of the fifth, which is designed to bring the lovers to a realization that never becomes as great as this, would be irrelevant. To follow the original development of the play, we must therefore confine our attention to the earlier version of his speech, concluding with the lines:

> Then when ourselves we see in ladies' eyes,
> Do we not likewise see our learning there?

This part is entirely in character; and without being profound, it is none the less a stage in the gradual deepening of the ideas of love and learning which Berowne was merely toying with in act one:

> Study me how to please the eye indeed,
> By fixing it upon a fairer eye—

He did this when he met Rosaline; and the consequences were so disturbing that he tried to defend himself from them by denigration—"two pitch-balls stuck in her face for eyes!" But nothing can save him from Shakespeare's decision that his understanding is due to be quickened. As he gazes into the balls of pitch, they are transmuted to crystal, in which he beholds a vision:

> From women's eyes this doctrine I derive:
> They are the ground, the books, the academes
> From whence doth spring the true Promethean
> fire.   IV. iii

It may be that one's sweetheart's eyes are a natural source of revelation; but Shakespeare is certainly not copying nature in this context; he is observing, without parody or satire, an established rite in the "religion" of love.

Quiller-Couch has remarked: "The reader who takes the trouble to go through *Love's Labour's Lost* marking every allusion to women's eyes will be positively confounded by their number until it breaks on him that however many, however puzzling, its separate topical riddles may be, here—and precisely here—lies the secret of the play." The final form of the play is concerned with a deeper secret; but eyes might have been the secret of the first version, to which it would have been appropriate. But a secret, even a little one, invites us to do more than take note of its existence, it requires penetration. Berowne derives his doctrine from Rosaline's eyes, but Shakespeare had it from other sources. It is worth while to take a glance at them, because this is not the only occasion on which their influence is considerable.

A possible source for the ritual of the eye is, once again, Chaucer's fragmentary translation of *The Romance of the Rose*. As this poem is cast in the form of a dream, we may call its young hero the dreamer, until, after being struck by the arrows, he becomes the lover. When he enters the garden of the Rose, he is invited to join the dance; and when that is over, he is left alone. The other dancers drift away in couples, and as he sees them go, he thinks that only a great fool would not long for such a life, since to have the love of one's choice is heaven:

> For better lyfe durst him not care
> For there nys so good paradyse
> As to haue a loue at his deuyse—   1326

47

He wanders through the garden alone; but all the while the god of love is stalking him, an arrow ready for his bow. The dreamer feels apprehensive at this; he senses that there may be more to love than delight, that there may be much peril in it and pain; and he prays that if the god should loose the arrow, it will not cause a mortal wound:

> Nowe god that sytteth in maieste
> Fro deedly woundes he kepe me
> If so be that he had me shete
> For if I with his arowe mete
> It had me greued sore ywis—   1343

It seems as if, like Berowne, he would prefer to take love lightly. When he has explored all the beauties of the garden, he comes to the spring of Narcissus, and again feels a pang of alarm. Narcissus was punished for selfishly withholding love, and the dreamer is at first reluctant to look into the water. Then he reassures himself that, as he is not disdainful, he will be in no danger, and he approaches the fountain. Whoever looks into it is sure to fall in love.

> For Venus sonne / dan Cupido
> Hath sowen there of loue the sede—   1617

Dan Cupid, we may notice in passing, is a somewhat uncommon title that Berowne also uses in recalling the moment when he was likewise smitten. The dreamer is now certainly in danger:

> And for the sede that here was sowen
> The welle is cleped / as is wel knowen
> The welle of Loue—   1627

He looks in; and at the bottom of the well he sees the two marvellous crystals that reflect and contain the whole garden in themselves. These are the lady's eyes, into which he gazes for a long while. A rose garden is revealed in their depths, and one of the rosebuds is particularly captivating:

> Whan I had smelled the sauour swote
> No wyl had I fro thence yet go—   1707

He is caught, first by the fascinating crystals and then by the perfume of the rosebud, her eyes and her love; so the god's moment has come, he looses his arrows— five of them—and the dreamer becomes the lover. Thereupon, as we have already noticed, it is not to the lady that he kneels, but to the god; and he receives, in a very long speech, Love's commandments, which are by no means easy to keep.

We might fairly say that, in the "religion" of love, the lady's eyes represent the baptismal font. And in Dante, for whom love takes on a mystical significance, which can hardly be attributed to *The Romance of the Rose*, this subtle meaning becomes more evident. I am not affirming that Shakespeare was directly influenced by Dante, but that both of them—together with Guillaume de Lorris, Chaucer and many more—were nourished by a common tradition, virtually a faith, to which each made a unique contribution. They share the idea that falling in love is something more than a romantic experience; it is also a rite of initiation into a new life.

On the first page of the *Vita Nuova*, Dante speaks of the moment—"When first the glorious Lady of my mind was made manifest to mine eyes."[1] And in association with this event, he tells us— "There is a rubric, saying, 'Here beginneth the New Life'—" *Incipit Vita Nova*. Since Dante's relations with Beatrice were always of "*fino amore*", imaginative and mystical, we may detect the baptismal nature of this experience more definitely than in that of the dreamer at the fountain. Dante was no doubt precocious in entering on this higher love-life at the age of nine! But he did not begin to write the *Vita Nuova* until he was twenty, and he was at least thirty before he finished it; so that the work itself, especially by the standards of poetic genius, is mature. As it proceeds, what we may call the ritual significance of the eye becomes even greater.

In the sonnet beginning:

Amore e 'l cor gentil sono una cosa,[2]

Dante introduces the theme of love as power. And explaining the sonnet himself, he says that in the first part—"I speak of him according to his power. In the second, I speak of him according as his power translates itself into act."[3] This theme he expands; and the following sonnet,

Negli occhi porta la mia donna Amore,[4]

is thus interpreted—"I say how this lady brings this power into action by those most noble features, her eyes; and . . . I say how she with power makes noble that which she looks upon; and this is as much as to say that she brings love, in power, thither where it is not . . . I say how she brings love, in act, into the hearts of

---

[1] *Dante's Vita Nuova with Rosetti's Version.* Chatto & Windus, 1908.
[2] *Ibid.,* p. 86. [3] *Ibid.,* p. 89. [4]*Ibid.,* p. 90.

all those whom she sees . . . I tell what she afterwards,
with virtue, operates upon their hearts."

Here, in extreme compression, as within a seed, is a
philosophy of love as a transforming principle—power,
act, and virtue. In *Love's Labour's Lost*, Shakespeare
announces in his own way (I do not imply a conscious
connection) the same theme, and he never forgot it; by
the time he comes to *Measure for Measure*, the theme is
in its third phase, forth-going virtue; and by this he
resolves tragedy. If, then, the lady's eyes are conceived
symbolically, as the font of love, where these tremendous
possibilities begin, they may well have been the point
of the earlier version of *Love's Labour's Lost*; and the
affirmation of love as power is, perhaps, the additional
point of the second version.

It is not necessary to affirm that Shakespeare was in
debt to Dante; nor need it be denied. The first printing
of the *Vita Nuova* was made in Florence in 1576. At
that time, when England was looking to Italy as the
land of culture, nothing that the Italian presses turned
out passed unnoticed. And in the cultivated circles
which Shakespeare undoubtedly frequented, he may
well have heard these fecund ideas discussed. I will not
rate this higher than a possibility, but that an idea that
has an affinity with Dante's was a dynamic part of his
own philosophy can, I think, be shown.

*   *   *

At the end of the fourth act, then, we may say—
irrespective of Dante—that the young men have
entered on a new life. The fact that they have done so in
a light-hearted manner does not make it less novel; but

as Shakespeare's intention is to bring the play to a serious conclusion—probably more serious in the second version than in the first—he must show this levity to be inadequate, and then change it into something else. At this time, perhaps, he had not himself experienced the torments of love that may change it into a destructive force; if that is so, part of the importance of these early plays may be that he is creating, in relative calm, an ideal to which he himself was able to hold when the storm broke on his own life. We have no biographical details; but his poetry is enough to tell us that he had lived through the hell as well as the heaven of the heart. Here, however, he seems to be personally at peace. And he ends the act with a glorious battlecry!

> LONGAVILLE: Shall we resolve to woo these girls of
> France?
> KING: And win them too. . . .
> BEROWNE: Advance your standards, and upon them,
> lords;
> Pell-mell, down with them!   IV. iii

But the girls of France are not to be conquered in this crude manner. Again, perhaps, Shakespeare is remembering the allegory of the Rose. Acceptance by the god of love is a privilege, and it is granted only under certain conditions:

> For curteys / and of fayre manere
> Wel taught / and ful of gentylnysse
> He muste ben / that shal me kysse—   2006
>
> And first of o thyng warne I the
> That payne and great aduersyte
> He mote endure / and eke trauayle
> That shal me serue / without fayle—   2012

In the fifth act, Shakespeare makes, in effect, the same stipulations. And he goes on to strip the last insincerities from love, in order that the quality itself may shine out clearly.

The young men begin by sending jewels to their ladies, accompanied by:

> —as much love in rhyme
> As would be cramm'd up in a sheet of paper,
> Writ o' both sides of the leaf, margent and all—

That will not pass; it is only good for laughter, and the girls dismiss it as:

> A huge translation of hypocrisy—   V. ii

The lords then come in person; but they are in disguise, dressed up as Russians. Clearly, this is part of a parable on semblance and reality. Boyet has heard the plan being hatched, and he warns the princess:

> Love doth approach disguised—

The penalty for this little trick is that the ladies also mask themselves, and exchange the jewels that have just been sent to them. When the men arrive, each woos the girl who is wearing his own gift, and so vows fidelity to the wrong one. The king proposes to Rosaline, assuming her to be the princess; and when asked why he thought her to be so, he replies:

> I knew her by the jewel on her sleeve.

They are all, in fact, making love to illusions; all—

> Following the signs, woo'd but the sign for she.

If we accept the hypothesis of the duality of Shakespeare's heroines, then the undermeaning of this

53

scene is clear: the young men do not yet know what love is. Their conception of it, and their courtship are those of the conventions, they are merely wooing the signs; and that, Shakespeare is saying, goes for the audience as well, until some awakening experience reveals the deeper truth. We should no doubt concede, in view of the diversity of love-conventions in different societies and periods, that this is so, and also that there is a permanent power in the background. Whether Shakespeare succeeded in elucidating its nature, or whether he merely arrayed it in a vision of his own, is another matter: all we can attempt to do is to establish what he believed himself to have discovered, and what he affirmed. It is at least certain that he pursued the enquiry with high seriousness—even in comedy— throughout his work, and reached some astonishing conclusions. And I am sure we ought to grant—as some critics do not—that Shakespeare was sincere.

*   *   *

Love's labour is lost in this play because it is a labour of affectation and not sincerity. But it will be won—so we are promised at the end—by service and sacrifice. Shakespeare is winnowing the chaff from the wheat. His present method of doing this is satirical: he makes the protestations of affectation ridiculous, and when they have been laughed off the stage, that which remains can be relied upon. At last, the characters begin to see into themselves; and this is so important to Shakespeare's future work that it must be stressed. Beneath the fancy-dress is the true self. And when this is revealed, it is not only the ladies who will be reassured: the lords will also have found something, hitherto unknown, that they can rely on in themselves. Their discovery is not, of course, complete; but it is towards this inner simplicity that they are tending:

> O, never will I trust to speeches penn'd,
>> Nor to the motion of a schoolboy's tongue;
> Nor never come in vizard to my friend;
>> Nor woo in rhyme, like a blind harper's song!
> Taffeta phrases, silken terms precise,
>> Three-pil'd hyperboles, spruce affectation,
> Figures pedantical; these summer-flies
>> Have blown me full of maggot ostentation;
> I do forswear them: and I here protest,
>> By this white glove,—how white the hand,
>> God knows!—
> Henceforth my wooing mind shall be express'd
>> In russet yeas, and honest kersey noes.   V. ii

That the way to love is to approach it sincerely might have made an adequate end. Could it have been the conclusion of the first version? What we naturally expect to happen is that the missing documents about Aquitaine should now be brought in, the negotiations between the king and princess be concluded, and that this agreement on affairs of state should be sealed by betrothals. That the earlier version did end something like this is suggested by the line in which the princess thanks the king:

> For my great suit so easily obtained.   V. ii

As the play stands, she has not obtained it: the business of her embassy is never referred to again. Shakespeare was notably careless in such matters; he often does not bother to delete an earlier line, but he could not have made her say such a thing in the first place without warrant. It is therefore fair to suspect that Mercade's original duty was to bring in the documents, and that in revising the play—there is plenty of evidence that the purpose of the revision was to deepen the thought— Shakespeare altered this to an announcement of death.

Death is not in keeping with the general temper of *Love's Labour's Lost*. But in Shakespeare's later work the death-shock is a device of the greatest significance. He makes regular use of it whenever a soul is to be turned from the descending to the ascending path. Confrontation with death is part of the shock-therapy of the Duke of Vienna; it is the stimulus to the conversion of Leontes; it is part of Prospero's purpose in managing the shipwreck; and it is surprising to meet with it in this early play. It strikes us here rather like hurling a thunderbolt to crush a thistle, but its function is comparable with that in the regeneration plays; and the probability that it has been inserted here, to give profundity to a work that was at first comparatively shallow, seems to me strong. However this may be, when Shakespeare uses the death-shock in such circumstances, we may be sure, by reason of many parallels, of what he has in mind: that one or more of his characters has come to a turning-point and is now to move through expiation to regeneration. This sounds altogether too portentous for a play like *Love's Labour's Lost*; the death-shock seems disproportionate, and from the point of view of aesthetic criticism we may be inclined to deprecate its use; but the incident is important in studying an aspect of Shakespeare that

is seldom recognized, namely, the ethical and philosophic unity of his whole work.

There are no unions of love at the end of this play;
but there is a promise of them, provided that love's
conditions are fulfilled. Here again, perhaps, there is
an influence from *The Romance of the Rose*. In that poem,
the lover yields unconditionally to the god, but he
does express the hope that finally he will be rewarded
with the Rose. The god then gives him encouragement:

> Loue sayde / dismay the nought
> Syth thou for socour hast me sought
> In thanke thy seruyce wol I take
> And highe of degree I wol the make— 2116

But the lover is warned that he must first learn to
wait and suffer; for without pain, no man comes to
bliss. Love must be trusted in spite of sorrow, for the
god knows how to cure the wound of his own arrows:

> Abyde and suffre thy distresse
> That hurteth nowe / it shal be lesse
> I wotte my selfe what maye the saue
> What medicyne thou woldest haue
>   And if thy trouthe to me thou kepe
> I shall vnto thyne helpyng eke
> To cure thy woundes— 2127

The winning of the Rose really depends on the lover
himself, on the quality of his service, and the sincerity
with which he keeps Love's commandments:

> For certainly thou shalte wel shewe
> Where that thou seruest with good wyl
> For to accomplysshen and fulfyl
> My comaundementes daye and nyght
> Which I to louers yeue of right. 2134

It is in this same spirit that Shakespeare ends *Love's Labour's Lost*; and as there are other reasons for supposing him to be indebted to *The Romance of the Rose*, it is fair to presume that he was influenced here. But there are also differences, which are equally important. The young men have to do the service or penances that their ladies place upon them, for a year and a day. The perfect fulfilment of these will win the Rose. The princess says to the king:

> Then, at the expiration of the year,
> Come, challenge me, challenge me by these
> deserts,
> And, by this virgin palm now kissing thine,
> I will be thine— V. ii

The essential idea is the same—the Rose of love is only to be won by service that is by no means easy to perform; but the character of the service is different. Although it would be incorrect to apply it to the whole, a part of the service in *The Romance of the Rose* might be termed dancing attendance on the lady. There is nothing of this in *Love's Labour's Lost*, the couples will not even meet until the term is over: the service, or penance, is wholly directed towards self-perfection. Once more we are made aware that Shakespeare is writing a parable, and that we are required to look deeper.

In *The Romance of the Rose*, the god of love goes on to deliver a long speech, more than a thousand lines, in the course of which he makes his commandments clear. This discourse, composed about the year 1230, might be regarded as an elementary text-book on courtly love, and Chaucer treated it as such. It influenced Shakespeare, but that did not prevent him from subjecting it to criticism and satire. Shakespeare never submitted to any influence with docility. There is no book, no dogma, no tradition—nothing that he took on trust. If it were possible to follow the advice of St Paul, and "test all things", he did so; and he held fast to what, in his own judgment, he found to be good. He therefore subjects the discourse of the god of love to a refining process in his own mind; he frequently satirizes those elements in it which he feels to be absurd, and retains what he believes to be its content of gold. In the same way that he is always close to the spirit of the Gospels, so he preserves the essence of the Rose: they are indistinguishable in his final plays; but he knew—it is part of his theory of tragedy—that the letter of the law, even of the highest law, kills.

*   *   *

Since we have the privilege of foreknowledge, we are entitled to use it; and doing so, we may pick out, at the beginning of Shakespeare's work, many seed ideas that prove to be viable. In the king's penance, I think there are two. The service that the princess requires of him, suggesting Delphi rather than Paphos, is this:

>   —go with speed
> To some forlorn and naked hermitage,
> Remote from all the pleasures of the world;
> There stay until the twelve celestial signs
> Have brought about the annual reckoning.
> If this austere insociable life
> Change not your offer made in heat of blood;
> If frosts and fasts, hard lodging and thin weeds

> Nip not the gaudy blossoms of your love,
> But that it bear this trial, and last love;
> Then, at the expiration of the year,
> Come challenge me—   V. ii

If we change our standpoint for a moment, and look back at this from the position of *Measure for Measure* or *The Tempest*, we are at once struck by the fact that the Duke of Vienna and Prospero—two heroes who had learnt in some degree to use the spiritual powers by which, and by nothing less, tragedy is resolved—both had had experience of "the life removed" that is now enjoined upon the king. Both had learnt in this eremitic phase to distinguish the false from the true, and had emerged from it not only with self-knowledge and a wider view of love, but as men of power. "By these deserts" they were able to challenge all things and snatch victory out of death. If we now turn back to the opening speech of *Love's Labour's Lost*, we shall find that that was exactly what the king was hoping to do— but by inadequate means. He says that in spite of devouring Time:

> The endeavour of this present breath may buy
> That honour which shall bate his scythe's keen
>   edge,
> And make us heirs of all eternity.   I. i

His method of attempting this was a vain one, as Berowne points out:

> So, ere you find where light in darkness lies,
> Your light grows dark by losing of your eyes.
>   I. i

But Berowne, at this stage, had not the correct answer either; his way to the stars was altogether too easy:

> —to study where I well may dine,
> When I to feast expressly am forbid;
> Or study where to meet some mistress fine,
> When mistresses from common sense are hid—
>   I. i

Our sympathies are enlisted for this point of view in
the first act; but Berowne is really only presenting the
obverse of the king's coin; and therefore, in the fifth
act, he is given a penance which is complementary to
that of the king. The king is to find the truth in solitude:
Berowne, who has already said that love is inseparable
from charity, is told by Rosaline:

> —to win me, if you please,
> Without the which I am not to be won,
> You shall this twelvemonth term from day to day
> Visit the speechless sick—   V. ii

He is to learn compassion, and to use his gift to help
instead of to hurt. Both these contrasting penances are
in the service of love, and their promised recompense
is the receiving of love's grace; but they will also result
in the expressing of love's power. On the evidence of
this play alone, we might suppose them to be alternative; but if we look ahead, we shall find them to be
successive. The Duke of Vienna, for instance, draws
these threads into a single pattern; having said:

> Heaven doth with us as we with torches do,
> Not light them for themselves; for if our virtues
> Did not go forth of us, 'twere all alike
> As if we had them not—   *M.M.* I. i

he then demonstrates in action that the torch which is
lit in solitude will shine out on the world.

The more we analyse the ethical implications of Shakespearean drama, the more it is revealed, in this respect, as a unity. It is certainly surprising that ideals which we might have thought belonged to his maturity are already emergent in *Love's Labour's Lost*. But they clearly are so. And we are confirmed in our previous surmise that his ideas at this period are far in advance of his power to express them dramatically: but that to do this—to use the stage for the dissemination of a highly individual, indeed a unique philosophy—was then, and never ceased to be, one of his intentions.

If Shakespeare ever did experience a "conversion"— a suggestion that has been put forward to explain his final plays—then it was not at the end, but at the beginning of his career. When the princess, after her death-shock, speaks "out of a new sad soul", our thoughts are directed towards serious things with as much insight as the author could, at that time, command. There is no literary posing in this, and it might reflect a personal experience. One of the strongest impressions the play leaves with us is sincerity. It is clear that Shakespeare is already interested in the problem of distinguishing between appearance and reality, he is trying to strip "the trappings and the suits" from "that within which passeth show", and a sojourn in the naked hermitage is merely a metaphor for undertaking this difficult work. That is why the princess's speech seems to have a Delphic tone; in under-meaning, her command is close to that inscribed on the temple. It is therefore related to Shakespeare's "dramatic" religion, which appears to rest upon four commandments: two from the Gospels; one from

Apollo's temple, "Know thyself"; and one of his own devising, that matches it, "To thine own self be true". We cannot know whether he tried to live by them; but I believe it will be shown that it was on this foundation that he built his plays.

As we try to follow his ideas, it is helpful to take note of the remarkable fluidity of his characters: the king and Berowne, as has been pointed out, are later integrated in the Duke of Vienna; and we must be prepared for others of this sort, for it is a part of his allegorical method. The Princess of France, and Jaquenetta, the peasant girl, both symbolize love as a transforming power; later on, we find their roles combining—the princess, the country maiden, and the goddess—in the person of Perdita, a figure of multiple allegory and also a channel of power, who, by her invocation to Proserpine, brings back the wasted beauty of the world.

*   *   *

Mention of Jaquenetta brings us to the sub-plot. This is of interest from so many points of view that to follow it in detail would lead to bewildering by-paths; we must therefore keep to its outlines. The development of Armado's love-affair with Jaquenetta presents, like the main plot, a gradual deepening of the idea of love: beginning in scorn, it ends in devotion. In his first confession, Armado says:

> I will hereupon confess I am in love; and as it is base for a soldier to love, so am I in love with a base wench. If drawing my sword against the humour of affection would deliver me—   I. ii

But it will not. Love is mightier than the sword; and it is not long before Armado admits as much:

> Adieu, valour! rust, rapier! be still, drum! for your manager is in love; yea, he loveth. Assist me some extemporal god of rhyme, for I am sure I shall turn sonnet. Devise, wit; write, pen; for I am for whole volumes in folio.   I. ii

Only the first page of these inspired works has been handed down to us; it is a letter to Jaquenetta, in which he writes:

> Shall I command thy love? I may: shall I enforce thy love? I could: shall I entreat thy love? I will. What shalt thou exchange for rags? robes; for tittles? titles; for thyself? me. Thus, expecting thy reply, I profane my lips on thy foot, my eyes on thy picture, and my heart on thy every part—   IV. i

At last, in the fifth act—but probably only in Shakespeare's second version of it—he discovers that there is a divinity in love, and that it does not profane, but sanctifies his lips to kiss in worship; so he declares:

> I am a votary; I have vowed to Jaquenetta to hold the plow for her sweet love three years.   V. ii

This is Shakespeare's way of showing how the sword shall be beaten into ploughshares, and this final touch may have been added when he was deepening the thought-content of the play. It seems hardly possible that he could have forgotten that Jaquenetta was in no condition to wait; he simply did not bother with such realistic trifles, once his new, important statement had been made.

64

Holofernes and Nathaniel are figures of fun; but even they, besides provoking laughter, are part of the "message" of the play. They have learning, and little else; they demonstrate how ineffectual learning by itself can be. But in Shakespeare's hands comedy is never unkind, and he uses them to make this point. In their absurd performance of the Nine Worthies, these secondary characters are baited and mocked by the rest; and as Holofernes makes his exit, wounded by this treatment, he exclaims:

> This is not generous, not gentle, not humble.
>
> V. ii

The judgment is certainly Shakespeare's; for the penances shortly to be imposed on the main characters will instil these qualities, incidentally, as part of the discovery of the true nature of love. And we are at once reminded that in *The Romance of the Rose* these were the virtues with which the lover had to begin. The god would not grant his kiss to anyone who was without them:

> For I am of the selfe manere
> Gentyll / curteys / meke / and fre.   2021

Shakespeare has turned the line into modern English.

The basic conflict, at the opening, was between learning and loving, with our sympathies enlisted on the side of love. But at the close, learning has not really suffered a defeat. Both these activities are stripped of affectation; and when the deeper character of each is thus laid bare, they are shown to be in harmony with one another and with life. When the curtain falls, the young men are about to enter on a new course of study. And it will be for the enhancement of life.

We may now briefly recapitulate some of the points which, having been established in this play, Shakespeare takes for granted in the future. He agrees with Dante, and other medieval poets, that love is "first learned in a lady's eyes". In the religion of love, they are the font. After this experience or rite, a new life begins; and one revelation of it—again he accords with Dante—is that love is power. In later work, Shakespeare fully recognizes that this power may be devastating; and in order that it shall be creative, a distinction must be made between the object of love and the ideal. The duality of Shakespearean heroines is, therefore, a principle; it is also a well-recognized allegorical device, long since established in the *Vita Nuova* and the *Roman de la Rose*. In this tradition, to court the lady is to worship the god, and this dual activity is implicit in the service of the Rose. If we accept, as I think we must, that Shakespeare is aware of this tradition, as well as that of Renaissance Platonism, and has adapted both to his own purposes, then we understand at once, in the tragedies, that when the heroine is misused, he is thereby telling us that a divine principle is being betrayed. That this principle ultimately resides in the hero's own self, and that the betrayal of it must result in his own destruction, are Shakespearean propositions, the establishing of which we must later attempt to trace.

Besides these general considerations, I should like to point to five fundamental ideas that we shall frequently re-encounter:

"LOVE'S LABOUR'S LOST"

(1) The condemning of one character by another
whose guilt is equal or greater. Armado and
Berowne both do this here in scenes of comedy,
but it is a situation that Shakespeare uses
regularly with most serious intention:

> Thieves for their robbery have authority
> When judges steal—   *M.M.* II. ii

(2) The gradual unveiling of reality, by the stripping
away of a multitude of disguises:

> —these indeed seem . . .
> But I have that within which passeth show;
> These but the trappings and the suits . . .
> *H.* I. ii

not of woe only, nor of love only, but of the
spirit.

(3) The confrontation with death as a turning-
point, at which the downward movement of a
character is checked and an ascent begun.

(4) The "naked hermitage" as a necessary phase in
the acquiring of self-knowledge.

(5) That the great aim is a synthesis of self-
knowledge and love.

Love's Labour's Lost ends, it has been gracefully
observed, in bird-calls. It should however be noticed
that these are ironic and not idyllic in character.

A good deal has been said of the inadequacy of mere
learning, and we conclude with lines that learned men
have composed in praise of the owl and the cuckoo—
the one, a bird whose wisdom is benighted, and the
other, whose love-life leaves much to be desired.

Chapter III

"THE ROMANCE OF THE ROSE"

W E shall have occasion to refer to the *Roman de la Rose* again; and for the sake of clarity, therefore, it will be well to consider the poem briefly in its own right. To do justice to it, in a short space, is impossible; and it must suffice if its salient features, and some points of special importance to our enquiry, are recalled.

The *Roman de la Rose* is the work of two poets, Guillaume de Lorris and Jean de Meun. Both came from the country of the Loire, and—if we may take Jean's word for it—the one died before the other was born. Guillaume tells us that he was twenty-five when he began the *Roman*. The date is uncertain, but it was at some time between 1225 and 1240. He left the work unfinished, and about forty years after his death, it was concluded—in a very different strain—by Jean de Meun. Their outlooks reflect the contrast between a chateau in the country and a study in the town. Guillaume's affinities are aristocratic; Jean's incline to be bourgeois, and although he was born near Orleans, he lived in the Faubourg Saint-Jacques and might even be acclaimed as the first Parisian intellectual. The date at which he began his continuation is not definitely known, but it is agreed that he was at work on it in the twelve-seventies. So he may have been labouring in his study on that May morning of 1274, when, far away in Florence, Dante saw Beatrice for the first time.

These three poets share the background of courtly love; but the effect it had on them—and they on it—is arrestingly dissimilar. One might say, to risk a generalization, that Guillaume treats this tradition aesthetically, Jean rationally and Dante spiritually. But we must not think of them as body, mind and spirit of the same idea; for while Guillaume and Dante are in sympathy with it, Jean is not.

In spite of much research, the origins of the medieval "religion" of love are still a challenge to the social historian. It has even been attributed to "Ovid misunderstood", but this is certainly inadequate. It is true, of course, that Ovid's theme of *quaerenda est puella* is one of perennial inspiration; and his reminder that she must be sought for, and will not come floating through the air—

> *haec tibi non tenues veniet delapsa per auras,*
> *quaerenda est—*

has delighted every age. But courtly love proved to be one of the greatest powers in the shaping of European social relations—its influence is with us still—and it is impossible to believe that it derived from a poem that is largely a *jeu d'esprit*; if we accepted that, then we might almost be prepared to credit that some future code of manners may rest on a misunderstanding of *The Importance of Being Earnest*. But it cannot be denied that the *Ars Amatoria* has a way of surprising us, in a frivolous context, with some penetrating shafts of thought; and perhaps it was not so much misunderstood in the Middle Ages as re-interpreted. Many of Ovid's ideas are susceptible of re-interpretation in a different social and religious setting. His remark, for example, that false love may sometimes become true—

fiet amor verus qui modo falsus erat—

is deeper than he would seem to have intended; and if mystically minded poets, particularly in the thirteenth century, took it in the sense that human love may become divine, then it at least suggests a link with Dante.

But whatever the causes of courtly love, the fact that it proved so successful shows that it answered to a psychological need; and we must locate this as much in the realm of religious as of social psychology. Between Eros and the spirit there is an unbreakable bond, but this may appear in a variety of shapes. The expression of it that took place in the course of the twelfth century had great social consequences, the most lasting of which was an immense improvement in the status of the weaker sex. To Aristotle, woman was inferior by nature[1]; to St Paul, she was so by the method and purpose of her creation;[2] and to many of the Christian Fathers she was an impediment to holiness, whom it was safer not to see. Then, almost suddenly it seems, as if invested with the aura of the vanished goddesses, she becomes an object of devotion, the means to a mystical revelation, and a radiant avenue to God:

O isplendor di viva luce eterna![3]

Dante exclaims, as the full vision of Beatrice breaks upon his sight. Those words, coming from the most

[1] *Politics*, I. v. 7.   [2] I Corinthians xi, 7-11.
[3] *Purgatorio*, xxxi, 139.

Christian of poets, would have scandalized the early saints. And they are clearly not derived from a superficial code of manners, but from activities of the soul that are religiously expressed.

I think it is important for us to recognize that the medieval "religion" of love was almost a faith in its own right, possessing a ritual and a code of morals, and able to induce the confirmatory experiences of mysticism and ecstasy; for although we may consider it irrational and absurd, it is not legitimate to call it blasphemy. Beatrice, first in body and then in spirit, led Dante by way of it to

> *luce intellettual piena d'amore,*[1]

or, as Cary at this point translates her:

> Forth from the last corporeal are we come
> Into the heaven, that is unbodied light;
> Light intellectual, replete with love;
> Love of true happiness, replete with joy;
> Joy, that transcends all sweetness of delight—

This is not the place, however, to discuss Dante, and I quote him only as an illustration of the possibilities of courtly love. He was not the only poet to realize them, nor the first. In a celebrated *canzone*, written when Dante was in his cradle, Guido Guinizelli reasons with God on the subject of his lady, and in the end he is justified. God says to him, "These praises that you sing to her belong to me—*a me convien la laude.*" And Guido answers, in effect, "It is true that all love comes from you, but your love is revealed to me through her.

---

[1] *Paradiso,* XXX, 40.

71

She comes to me as an angel from your presence.
Blame me not, then, if I love her."

> *Dir li potrò: "Tenne d'angel sembianza*
> *Che fosse del tuo regno:*
> *Non mi fu fallo s'eo le posi amanza."*[1]

Guido's three lines show us a seed-thought of Dante's
thousands; and in the sonnets of Michelangelo,
written three centuries later, the idea has lost nothing
of its vitality: the beloved is—or rather, she may be—
an angelic messenger, who brings the divine love down
to earth. It is not essential that she should be conscious
of her role; the spiritual perception is in the lover, to
whom it may bring an overwhelming experience, "*Ecce
Deus fortior me, qui veniens dominabitur mihi.*"[2] It is
surely not irrelevant that besides its supreme poets the
thirteenth century was remarkable for its mystics; and
that Eckhart was contemporary with Dante.

*   *   *

The *Roman de la Rose*, to which we must now return,
does not approach these heights; and Jean de Meun, at
least, had no conception of their existence. Perhaps its
limitations were conducive to its immense success. For
three centuries it was a widely read and influential work;
even so, it is astonishing that more than three hundred
manuscripts still survive. Chaucer tells us, in the
prologue to *The Legend of Good Women*, that he translated it. If he translated the whole, which is unlikely
then his version has perished. What we now possess in

---

[1] This *canzone* will be found in *The Oxford Book of Italian Verse*,
page 70.
[2] Dante, *Vita Nuova*.

Middle English is three fragments—seven thousand six hundred and ninety-eight lines in all. A part of the first fragment is probably by Chaucer, and all of them are included in his collected works. It was from these fragments that the *Roman* was known to English readers in the sixteenth century. They were first printed by William Thynne in 1532, under the title of *The Romaunt of the Rose*,[1] and it is from this edition that I shall continue to quote.

The courtship of the Rose, as Guillaume de Lorris relates it, is a dream. But it is not a naturalistic one, for dream-poetry in the Middle Ages was a literary form with its own conventions. It is a form that is quite lost to contemporary poetry, and perhaps the only art that could bring it to life for us today is the ballet. This may sound a strained comparison; and yet I believe Guillaume's part of the story would make a delightful ballet, and the two art-forms have several qualities in common. To think of *Swan Lake* or *Les Sylphides* is enough to remind us how easily ballet slips into a world of dream, allegory and romance, and yet always retains the lucid wakefulness of finely disciplined and highly stylized art. I do not wish to press the analogy unduly; but these are precisely the qualities that Guillaume de Lorris displays, and his kind of poetry, also like the ballet, was originally a courtly creation, addressed to the most cultivated minds of the age. The appreciating of such art is rather like a love-affair—mere passivity on one side will not do; it requires creative activity in the audience as well as in the artist.

[1] The line-numbering is the same in the Oxford ed. of *The Complete Works of Chaucer*.

Guillaume's story is told in the first person. The lover, who is also the narrator, begins by saying that he believes some dreams to be of great importance, and even prophetic. And he proposes to recount to us one of his own, which time fulfilled. He is doing this in honour of someone who is so precious that she is herself worthy to be called the Rose.

In his dream, he finds himself beside a river, on a morning in May. It is the clear river of life. He gazes into it with delight, stoops to bathe his face in the fresh water, and then walks along the bank. Presently he sees a high wall surrounding a garden—it is really love's garden, which at his age he ought to enter—but he sees no gate. So he wanders round the wall.

On the outside of this, a number of unpleasant allegorical figures are painted; they stand for the qualities and conditions that are impermissible in an ideal lover, and that is what the young dreamer is aspiring to be. The qualities, unless we include Sorrow among them, are all vicious: Hatred, Covetousness, Averice, Envy, Felony, Villainy and Pope Holy—the last meaning pharisaical piety seeking the praise of men instead of the grace of God. We are given lively sketches of them all—Averice, for example, dressed in rags,

> As she were al with dogges torne
> And both behynde and eke beforne—   222

The conditions are merely pitiful—penury and old age:

> But nathelesse I trowe that she
> Was fayre somtyme / and fresshe to se—   404

Neither of these need be a barrier to spiritual love—and when Jean de Meun takes over the poem, he goes out of his way to praise both; but they are clearly not compatible with a perfect courtship.

* * *

It is necessary to remember that the lover is dreaming. The garden of the Rose is not a place, but a state of mind. It is what every imaginative youth discovers when he has the leisure to dream; but it cannot be explored by a young man in a hurry. The first gift that the Rose expects of him is his time. And so when the dreamer finds a gate in the wall, and knocks, it is opened by a lovely creature named *Oiseuse*, or Idelnesse. She has golden hair, arched eyebrows, a dimpled chin, and

> There nys a fayrer necke iwys
> To fele howe smothe and softe it is
> Her throte also whyte of hewe
> As snowe on braunche snowed newe— 558
>
> And for to kepe her hondes fayre
> Of gloues whyte she had a payre. 572

She is, in fact, beautifully turned out, wearing a little coronet, and a garland of roses. *Oiseuse* had no thought in life but to look attractive; so when she had combed her hair, and dressed herself to perfection, her work was done:

> *Quant ele s'estoit bien pigniee,*
> *E bien paree e atornee,*
> *Ele avoit faite sa jornee.*[1]   II. 570

[1] French quotations from *Le Roman de la Rose* are from the edition of Langlois, published by the *Société des Anciens Textes Français*, five vols., Paris 1914-1924. The first vol. is introductory. My references are to volume and line.

She does, however, give herself the trouble to open the gate, and to tell the dreamer that the garden belongs to *Deduiz*—in the English version, Myrthe; then she leaves him to his own discoveries, which are, in a way, self-discoveries. The garden is so enchanting that it seems to him an earthly paradise:

> So fayre it was / that trusteth well
> It semed a place espyrituell— 650

We feel that we have entered the poets' paradise, that is not so much to come, as ever present; it is the existing world around us transfigured by the imagination; and all the romantic poets rediscover it. Only the décor changes with the age. In this garden, where the trees and flowers are described with that sensitivity to detail that the pre-Raphaelites attempted to recapture, the birds sing lays and sonnets in the service of courtly love:

> *Grant servise douz e plaisant*
> *Aloient li oisel faisant;*
> *Lais d'amors e sonez cortois*
> *Chantoient en lor serventois,*
> *Li un en haut, li autre en bas.* II. 705

In fact our dreamer has given a period costume to an ageless inner world; and this he continues to do, when he meets the lord of the garden, Myrthe, and his guests. He finds them dancing a *querole*, in which Lady Curtesye at once invites him to join:

> A lady gan me for to espye
> And she was cleped Curtesye
> The worshypful / the debonayre
> I pray to god euer fall her fayre
> Ful curteysly she called me
> What do ye there Beau sire (qd she)

76

Come / and if it lyke you
To daunsen / daunseth with vs now——   802

He does so, and describes the company. We see at once
that it represents the qualities and conditions that are
the opposite of the grim paintings on the outside wall.
In place of Elde, there is Youthe—just a happy child,
who has not a thought of harm or an evil design in her
head:

> Nicete fu, si ne pensoit
> Nul mal ne nul engin qui soit——   II. 1264

The rest are all presented as fair ladies: Rychesse,
Largesse, Fraunchise, Curtesye, Beautie, and, of
course, leisure, *la bele Oiseuse*, without whom the
dreamer would never have managed to get in. Each is
characterized in detail which we need not follow here.
But the most important person is the god of love. He,
too, is an ageless idea in a period dress; and his literary
significance in this form is great. Although he is armed
with a bow—or, to be more exact, he has an attendant
who carries two—he is otherwise quite different from
Cupid. There is nothing childish about him. He is a
fair young man. He appears in Chaucer, almost in his
present form, notably in the prologue to *The Legend of
Good Women*; and he is also no doubt related to the
one-time consort of the Queen of May. Here, he is
clothed in a marvellous living robe of flowers:

> His beutie greatly was to prise
> But of his robe to deuyse
> I drede encombred for to be
> For not ycladde in sylke was he
> But al in floures and flourettes
> Ypaynted al with amorettes——   892

77

Round his head, there is a perpetual fluttering of birds
—nightingales, popinjays, larks; and he himself seems
like an angel come fresh from heaven:

> *Qu'il estoit toz coverz d'oisiaus,*
> *De papegauz, de rossigniaus,*
> *De calandres e de mesenges.*
> *Il sembloit que ce fust uns anges*
> *Qui fust tot droit venuz dou ciel.*　　II. 903

Perhaps he inspired the "winged messenger of heaven"
whom Romeo imagines. He has with him a squire,
named *Douz Regarz*, or Swete Lokyng, who carries
two bows and ten arrows. One of the bows is beautifully
made, and the five arrows that fit it are golden; the
other is black and ugly, made from a tree that bears an
evil fruit:

> Ful croked was that foule stycke
> And knotty here and there also—　　927

And the appropriate arrows go with this, "blacke as
fende in hell". The arrows all have their names; but the
general contrast between the two quiversful is like that
between the paintings on the wall and the persons in
the dance: one group represents the incentives to love
that lead to the right service of the Rose, and the other,
those that do not.

When the *querole* is finished and the dancers dis-
perse, the dreamer begins to explore the garden, and
gives us a minute description of its beauties; all the
while, the god of love is following:

> *Li deus d'Amors tantost de loing*
> *Me prist a sivre, l'arc ou poing.*　　II. 1314

We have already touched on his experiences at the fountain, where he looks into the twin crystals and is struck by the five gold arrows. Then he yields to the god, as he ought, and receives the divine kiss and the commandments. And we have also noticed that the service of the Rose is not a series of selfish satisfactions, although there are many delights in the course of it; essentially it is a way of self-giving. So the lover surrenders his heart to the god, who locks it with his golden key:

> And hole myne herte taken me fro
> That it wol do for me nothyng
> But if it be at your byddyng
> Myn herte is yours / & myn right nought
> As it behoueth / in dede and thought— 2072

Having made due acknowledgement of the god, who then disappears, the lover naturally turns to the lady. And here we may wonder whether it is she herself, or her love, that is really the Rose. There is some ambiguity about this. In the deeper sense, the Rose is her love; but the whole poem is an offering to the dreamer's sweetheart:

> *Cele por cui je l'ai empris;*
> *C'est cele qui tant a de pris*
> *E tant est dine d'estre amee*
> *Qu'el doit estre Rose clamee.* II. 44

So it seems that the Rose may be both; but it is less often the person than the quality, and in general we must picture it as the lady's love. It is that, and not her person only, that must be won.

*   *   *

Between the lover and the Rose is the thorny hedge of social convention; and to find the right way through this, to a more intimate relationship, is his first problem. The correct approach is to observe the commandments he has just been given; but it is human to err, and he sometimes does.

His advances naturally provoke various reactions in the lady herself, and in the people round her. These states of mind and feeling are personified. Some favour the lover, some oppose him; and the interplay between these lively figures enables us to watch the emotional drama that is being enacted in her heart. In a sense, she is being psycho-analysed, and her inner life presented as a play; we never meet her as a complete person; but her emotions are introduced to us individually. From the point of view of literary technique, this type of allegory is of great importance; by imitation and development it was perpetuated; no later medieval poet escaped its influence, and I believe it is still discernible in Shakespeare. The first encounters between the lover and the lady may be sketched as an illustration of the allegorical method.

They meet; but there is no description of her. Instead, a handsome young man steps into the poem, and comes to greet the lover. His name is *Bel Acueil*— Bialacoil, in the English; he is the son of Curtesye, and represents the most gracious aspect of the lady's character—partly innate and partly born of her good manners. He favours the lover from the beginning, and is indispensable to his ultimate success. Almost at once, he invites him to pass through the outer hedge and enjoy the scent of the Rose, telling him that no

harm will come of that, provided always that he behaves
sensibly:

> *E me dist amiablement:*
> *"Biaus amis chiers, se il vos plaist,*
> *Passez la haie senz arest,*
> *Pour l'odor des roses sentir;*
> *Je vos i puis bien garantir*
> *N'i avroiz mal ne vilanie,*
> *Por quoi vos gardez de folie—"*   II. 2802

The lover has made an excellent start, but he tries to
force the pace too quickly. He tells Bialacoil that he is
in love, and that nothing will heal the wounds of the
god's five arrows except possession of the blossom:

> In me fyue woundes dyd he make
> The sore of whiche shal neuer slake
> But ye the bothom graunt me
> Whiche is moste passaunt of beaute
> My lyfe / my dethe / and my martyre
> And tresour / that I most desyre.   3112

This frightens Bialacoil, and he answers with spirit:

> A mokel foole than I were
> If I suffred you away to bere
> The fresshe bothom / so fayre of syght
> For it were neyther skyll ne right—   3120

The lover has blundered; and Bialacoil is effaced by a
very different mood, personified as *Dangiers*, or
Daungere, who chases the lover outside the hedge.
Daungere, who has been lying in ambush all the time,
is described as a huge, black, fire-eyed villain, whose
business it is to see that no man plucks the Rose. He
represents the lady's sense of outrage, expressed in
anger and haughty rebuff. He turns furiously on

Bialacoil; which means, of course, that she first blames herself for allowing the young man to grow too familiar. Then he rounds on the lover, "Flye hence, felowe!" And there is nothing to be done but go.

This is their first meeting. On the surface, it is a scene between three male characters. But the allegory is transparent, and has already told us a great deal about the lady. In principle, this is an art of telling two stories at once, as a parable does. The medieval love of dreams favoured its development by laying emphasis on the inner life; but the outcome is by no means vaguely dreamy. On the contrary, it is near to revealing the true springs of action, which are always the interplay of psychological forces working *as if* they were independent entities. What Guillaume de Lorris bequeathed to his successors was, in fact, an extremely subtle form of character-analysis; and the printing of *The Romaunt of the Rose*, in 1532, kept its memory green.

The lover, rebuffed and miserable, now lingers outside the hedge. Being a young man of intelligence as well as sensibility, he wonders if he is making a fool of himself. He tries to weigh up the situation. And this mental activity is displayed to us as a descent from her high tower of Lady Reason. She is a queenly personage, beyond the compass of unaided nature, and therefore heaven-born. She is neither old nor young—

> Ne hygh ne lowe / ne fatte ne lene
> But best / as it were in a mene
> Her eyen two were clere and lyght
> As any candell / that brenneth bright
> And on her heed she had a crowne
> Her semed wel an hygh person . . .

82

> Her goodly semblant by deuyse
> I trowe was made in paradyse
> For nature had neuer suche a grace
> To forge a werke of suche compace—   3208

She is able to give advice that will save all men from folly; but she cannot compel them to take it. She presents the facts, and tries to persuade her hearers to comply with them. "Thou haste bought dere the tyme of May," she tells the lover; and she assures him that his only hope of recovery is to transfer his allegiance from the god of love to herself:

> The god of Loue holly foryete
> That hath the in such payne sette—   3246

Clearly, after the vows he has just made, this would be a treacherous apostasy. Lady Reason seems singularly unconcerned about this moral problem; and when he rejects her counsel, she goes back, for the time being, to her tower.

No reader can fail to pause for reflection at this point. Guillaume de Lorris was an influential poet; and if he poses a moral problem, it must be faced. Love and Reason are presented here as antagonistic; and when the poem is taken over by its second author, their conflict is accentuated. There never is any reconcilement between them in *The Romance of the Rose*. A disputatious age might be content to leave the question open and to continue the argument; but the challenge of finding an acceptable solution remains; and to the Renaissance ideal of completeness, such an unbridged chasm was an offence. A "perfect man" cannot be psychologically split between Reason, the highest faculty, and Love, the sovereign good. For the analysis of character, of course, they must be separated; but when the goal is self-unity, integration becomes imperative. In a general sense, the Renaissance tends to view man as a complete being; many writers exemplify this, and Shakespeare does so pre-eminently. If he read *The Romaunt of the Rose*, this unresolved conflict would surely have challenged him. And it may be that the synthesis between love and learning, in *Love's Labour's Lost*, is a part of his reaction. When Reason next appears, as we shall see, she presents another pair of unreconciled opposites: love, as the lover understands it, and friendship. And it is precisely the harmonizing of these that Shakespeare undertakes in *The Two Gentlemen of Verona*. It is possible, of course, that the influence on him is indirect; but even if this is so, it is still noteworthy that a number of subjects that are presented in *The Romaunt of the Rose* in analysis are rehandled by Shakespeare in synthesis.

In his previous discourse, the god had advised the lover to have a confidential friend; and this important character now appears. He is most encouraging; and with his help, the lover makes his peace with Daungere. This readmits him to the lady's presence, but only on the formal side of the hedge. His evident unhappiness, however, soon touches her heart; and these stirrings of compassion are displayed to us analytically. Her personified emotions enact a scene. The characters are Daungere, Fraunchise and Pyte. Fraunchise is not easy to define; she stands for a quality that derives from being free-born, and so puts her case mainly from the standpoint of what a lady ought to feel and do.

"Daungere," she says, "you are too hard on this lover; it is unmannerly of you. He has not done any harm that I can see. And it is not for you to blame him for serving the god of love. He cannot do otherwise. Are you tormenting him simply because he is in your power? That would be disgraceful."

> *Mout a dur cuer qui ne se ploie*
> *Quant il trueve qui le souploie.*   II. 3284

Then Pyte speaks. Daungere has to give in. And Fraunchise sends back Bialacoil. All is now well again, perhaps even better than it was; and the lover asks Bialacoil if he may kiss the Rose. Bialacoil replies that he would not himself forbid it, but he is afraid of Chastyte:

> Thou shuldest nat warned be for me
> But I dare nat for Chastyte—   3670

She has forbidden kissing, because it is too nearly a promise of something more:

> For who so kyssynge maye attayne
> Of loues payne hath (sothe to sayne)
> The best and most auenaunt
> And ernest of the remenaunt.   3680

At this moment, however, Venus appears; or, to say it more simply, the lady's longing to be kissed becomes irresistible. Venus is carrying a lighted torch, which has the property of setting lovers on fire:

> This lady brought in her right honde
> Of brennynge fyre a blasyng bronde
> Wherof the flame and hote fyre
> Hath many a lady in desyre
> Of Loue brought—   3709

85

Venus speaks coaxingly to Bialacoil, and the lover is granted his kiss:

> *Un baisier douz e savoré.*   II. 3478

But the memory of this happiness has to suffice him for a long while, because the kiss has been noticed. *Male Bouche*, or Wicked Tonge, immediately starts talking. His poisonous gossip calls forth two of love's worst enemies—Shame, in the lady herself, and Jelousye, in her guardians. Jelousye rounds furiously on poor Bialacoil, and condemns him to be bound and shut up in a high tower:

> Great faute in the nowe haue I founde
> By god anone thou shalte be bounde
> And faste loken in a toure
> Without refuyte or socoure.   3840

In other words, she is never to smile at the young man again; and Daungere is summoned to throw him out of the garden.

*   *   *

At this moment of reversed fortunes, the work of Guillaume de Lorris ends. What became of him is not known; nor have we any certain knowledge of how he would have ended the poem. The opinions of experts differ, so we may guess what we please. One thing only is beyond doubt: he would not have finished it in the heretical manner of Jean de Meun. But to be concluded —in more than seventeen thousand lines—by a man who disbelieved in every ideal that the original stood for, was the curious fate of the *Roman de la Rose*.

This literary partnership, if such it may be called, between two men who never met, is one of the most incongruous imaginable; and the effect of it is rather stimulating. It is somewhat as if Keats had broken off early in *Endymion,* and the poem had been finished at prodigious length by Bernard Shaw—including all the *Prefaces* in verse. Like Shaw, Jean de Meun is determined to be didactic; and they equally regret the fact that if adults are to be effectively taught, a certain amount of time must be wasted in entertaining them. Both have a brilliant literary gift, and sugar their pill with sufficient story to keep an unstudious reader to his task. But the preface is the purpose of the play, and Jean continues the romance for the sake of his digressions. But he handles the love-story in a sly way, which has the effect of "debunking" the romantic ideal.

He does not understand the "religion" of love, and he dislikes it. From the idealistic point of view, his concluding lines are the height of cynicism: the lover not only wins the Rose, but several others. No wonder Chaucer was reprimanded by the god for translating such blasphemy! But once we have understood what is not to be expected of Jean de Meun, there is much to be said in his favour. First of all, he is honest. He believes what he says; and it is a part of his belief that to strip the falsity—as he conceives it—from thought and conduct is a moral obligation. He does this with a heavy hand, which sometimes strips the leaves from the plant; but we may respect his good intention. And it is precisely his zest for satirizing the meretricious in the interest of deeper values that may have been stimulating to Shakespeare.

It would be fair, I think, to consider Guillaume's conception of love as perfect romance; it is never coarse, and it is never, like Dante, mystical. Shakespeare was in sympathy with love of this kind, but it does not suffice him: he goes beyond it in both directions, higher and lower. And it is not impossible that he was encouraged by Jean's example. Jean is neither romantic nor mystical; he is sometimes coarse, but he is also very thoughtful. He likes to classify. And using Lady Reason as his mouthpiece, he divides love, as he understands that term, into its kinds, and explains them. The lover must have felt bewildered by this abrupt change in the character of his guide, or, one might say, of himself; for he began as an aspect of the soul of a poet, and he has now become an attentive student being lectured by a professor.

We left him in a miserable condition, having just been chased out of the garden. Guillaume, perhaps, would have brought Hope to comfort him: Jean, characteristically, brings the thought of Hope to torment him. It is impossible to abandon Hope; but hopeful people, he reflects, often come to a bad end:

> Her counsayle foly is to take
> For many tymes / whan she wol make
> A ful good sylogisme / I drede
> That afterwarde there shal in dede
> Folowe an euel conclusyoun
> This putte me in confusyoun—   4460

So the lover has begun to think in syllogisms, and the birds, we shall find, have ceased to sing sonnets. The climate of thought has violently altered. It is no longer determined by the imagination, but by the intellect. And presently, inevitably, Lady Reason comes down again from her tower:

> *"Beaus amis", dist Raison la bele,*
> *"Coment se porte la querele?*
> *Seras tu ja d'amer lassez?*
> *N'as tu pas eu mal assez?"*   II. 4232

In Guillaume's hands, she had not been very convincing, and had spoken at moderate length. But now, her arguments are powerful, and she holds the poem for three thousand and one lines. She fails, in the end, to win over the exhausted lover; but it is plainly Jean's opinion that nothing but his own folly is to blame for that.

Lady Reason does not confine herself to logic. She opens her discourse with a lecture on the irrationality of love, and immediately proposes to explain the inexplicable:

> *Or te demonterrai senz fable*
> *Chose qui n'est pas demonstrable—*   II. 4280

And she does so in a cataract of paradoxes, by which Romeo, it may be, was slightly splashed. Romeo, it will be remembered, launches himself with the line, "Why then, O brawling love! O loving hate!" And Jean de Meun's Reason begins:

> *Amour ce est pais haineuse,*
> *Amour c'est haine amoureuse—*   II. 4293

She cannot attain to Romeo's poetry, but her staying-power is considerably more. From the warning couplet,

> Nowe sette wel thyne ententioun
> To here of Loue discriptioun,   4702

there are eighty-one lines on love's paradoxical nature— a pious felony, a heavy burden light to carry, laughter that is always weeping, rest that labours day and night, the wearing of rags with golden lace. . . . Reason finally implies that love is inescapable, but it ought to be avoided. And the bewildered lover is no wiser than he was:

> "*Dame*", *fis je*, "*de ce me vant,*
> *Je n'en sai pas plus que devant—*"   II. 4362

He begs her to be plainer. And she agrees to put it simply: love is a mental illness afflicting two persons of opposite sex; it springs from an inordinate desire to kiss and embrace, and its aim is pleasure:

> More for delectatioun
> Than any procreatioun—   4822

And that, in Reason's view, is what is wrong. Procreation is necessary, but delectation—

> Suche loue I preyse nat at a leke.   4830

Once again, the analysis presents us—and leaves us—with a pair of unreconciled opposites. But creation and delectation are inseparable in life, and to put them asunder is imperfect in philosophy. When no link is admitted between the senses and the spirit, the idea of pleasure does indeed become debased; and it is significant that, in a later passage, Jean de Meun makes his lover condone promiscuity. Shakespeare never does. His love-plays close the chasm between body and spirit.

Apparently it does not occur to Jean de Meun that there might be a possibility of harmonizing the opposites. He stands on the indisputable fact that vicious love and virtuous love both exist in practice; and he subjects each sort to a searching analysis.

Reason, therefore, now informs the lover that although he is wrong to court the Rose, there are other varieties of love that are commendable. The first of these, she says, is friendship; and this leads her to an argument of great literary importance:

> Loue of frendshippe also there is
> Whiche maketh no man done amys
> Of wyl knytte betwixte two
> That wol nat breke for wele ne wo——   5204

In his methodical way, Jean deals with love in the form of friendship. He is a great collector of ideas, less often an originator of them, and most of what he says is drawn from Cicero's *De Amicitia*. The view that love between friends is superior to that between the sexes was widely held in the Middle Ages, as it was in antiquity. Its requirements were high. True friends were to have one purse and one mind between them, keeping neither wealth nor secrets from each other. Both the favours and the ill-turns of fortune were likewise to be divided; and of these two, the reverses were the better, for it was they that brought the proof of love. Jean has culled these ideas from the classics, and only his way of saying them is new. What is more remarkable is the stress he lays on the antagonism between this kind of love and the service of the Rose. The lover is advised to embrace the one and reject the other entirely:

> This loue that I haue tolde to the
> Is no thyng contrarye to me
> This wol I that thou folowe wele
> And leaue the tother euery dele——   5308

Now the alleged antagonism between these varieties of love is Shakespeare's theme in *The Two Gentlemen of Verona*; and his aim is to resolve the conflict. Whatever directed his attention to this subject, it is curious that in his next love-play he should again be preoccupied with a theme from *The Romaunt of the Rose*.

The discourse of Lady Reason next deals with the pursuit and accumulation of money. She is against both; because they spring from the false notion that earth and human limitations are man's true state, whereas, in her view, his real destiny is *"pure deité"*, and she quotes Pythagoras to support her:

> Pythagoras him selfe reherses
> In a booke that the golden verses
> Is cleped / for the nobilyte
> Of the honorable dyte
>   Than whan thou gost thy body fro
> Free in the eir thou shalte vp go
> And leauen al humanyte
> And purely lyue in deite
> He is a foole withouten were
> That troweth haue his countrey here.   5658

So the pursuit of wealth is folly, and the avaricious retention of it a sign of inward poverty; for it is lack of love—as she has defined it—that makes men avaricious:

> And in defaute of loue it is
> As it sheweth ful wel ywis
> For if these gredy / the sothe to sayne
> Loueden / and were loued agayne
> And good loue reigned ouer alle
> Suche wickednesse ne shulde fall
> But he shulde yeue / that moste good had

92

To hem that weren in nede bestad
And lyue without false vsure
For charyte / ful clene and pure—   5798

For Shakespeare, it is not merely avarice, but tragedy itself that springs from "defaute of loue". And it seems not unlikely that he read and took these lines to heart.

*   *   *

At this point there is a gap in the received text of the English version equivalent to nearly five thousand lines of the French. It would not have been difficult for Shakespeare to have had knowledge of its contents— at least fifteen editions of the French text had been printed before 1538, so that few books of comparable length were so widely known—but I shall not assume that he had. There is, however, one further point in the discourse of Lady Reason that would have been of great interest to him. The lover raises the question of the relation of love to justice, and asks her which is the better. There is no problem with which Shakespeare was more deeply concerned. His final answer to it goes beyond that of Jean de Meun, but in principle they agree. Lady Reason affirms that love is the better; because if love were to withdraw from the world, justice would destroy too much; but if justice were to depart, love alone would be able to make life good and beautiful:

> *Se Joustice iert toujourz gisanz,*
> *Si serait Amour soufisanz*
> *A mener bele vie e bone,*
> *Senz jousticier nule persone;*
> *Mais senz Amour Joustice non.*   II. 5531

Shakespeare goes all the way with Jean de Meun in this argument, and then a step further: he conceives love to be a regenerating power.

The further contents of the gap need not be dwelt on here. The lover decides to continue his courtship. Lady Reason leaves him, and Friend returns. The most significant part of Friend's advice is that he should have recourse to deceit. The service that Guillaume de Lorris first presented as an ideal, Jean de Meun is now turning into an intrigue; and his ulterior motive is evidently to discredit the whole affair. From the point of view of the "religion" of love, he is, as Chaucer says, a heretic; but all true heretics are reformers in their own eyes, and that is presumably what he felt himself to be.

The principle of deception, introduced by Friend, is later developed by the god of love in person. When the god reappears, he promises to bring all his forces to the lover's aid. The plan is to storm the fortress-tower in which Bialacoil is imprisoned. And the spearhead of the attack is False Semblant, who is the personification of deceit.

Guillaume would never have allowed the god of love to take False Semblant into his service; but he now becomes the principal character for Jean. When the English version takes up the story again, False Semblant delivers a very long speech. It has nothing to do with the action; ostensibly, it is to introduce and describe himself; in effect, it is an exposure of deceit in general, and in particular of hypocrisy disguised in holy orders:

> *La robe ne fait pas le moine.*   III. 11058

But False Semblant is everywhere. A part of his speech is a dissertation on disguises, a subject of life-long interest to Shakespeare:

> Ful wel I canne my clothes chaunge
> Take one / and make another straunge—

But Jean, again like Shakespeare, is concerned with the underlying truth to which dress is irrelevant, neither giving nor taking anything.

> *Bons cueurs fait la pensee bone,*
> *La robe n'i tost ne ne done.*   III. 11118

It would lead too far from our subject to follow the whole poem. The only other character in it who might be relevant to Shakespeare is the Vekke. Part of the advice she gives to Bialacoil is like that which Juliet received from her nurse, and which Juliet instantly rejected—"Ancient damnation!" Bialacoil's reaction is the opposite: he takes her poison drop by drop.

Jean makes vast digressions that have no connection with the story, and are devoted to expounding the science of the age. When at last he comes back to the liberation of Bialacoil, the prison-tower is stormed by Love's army; and by means of the fire-brand of Venus, it is taken. But in the sense in which Guillaume de Lorris began his poem, the lover never wins the Rose. Jean de Meun's ending is something very different—a successful seduction, promptly followed by two more:

> *Par grant jolieté coilli*
> *La fleur dou bel rosier foilli,*
> *Ainsinc oi la rose vermeille.*   V. 21779

This indiscriminate rose-gathering is no victory for the god of love; for he "loued neuer doublenesse". It is a violation of his law:

> And for thou trewe to loue shalt be
> I wyl / and comaunde the
> That in one place thou set al hole
> Thyn herte— 2364

In Jean's conclusion, False Semblant has taken all. He has entered into the lover and corrupted him, but his own character has not changed a jot. And in the last lines, he peeps from behind a new disguise with his familiar wink and snigger.

But Jean de Meun has honest intentions, and it would be wrong to blame him for debasing an ideal which he never understood. At its worldly best—disregarding its mystical side—courtly love is a process of refinement; and the ideal courtship of the Rose is, I think, an attempt to create a perfect human relationship. In this sense, it is—or it would be if achieved—a supreme work of art. Jean misses this point. But he does, following Cicero and the Gospels, present us with another ideal—antagonistic, in his view—that of a perfect relationship between friends.

This raises some questions. Is either of these ideals possible to attain? How do they stand to one another? Can they be embraced in a wider sphere of harmony? I will not say that Shakespeare formulated exactly these thoughts; nor, even if he did, that he was impelled to do so by *The Romaunt of the Rose*. But he deals with the same problems; he finds new answers to them; and we shall understand this achievement better against the background of the Rose.

We ought now to follow, link by link, the English chain of love philosophy between the *Roman* and Shakespeare—the contribution of Chaucer, Gower's *Confessio Amantis*, Usk's *Testament of Love*, and so on to Spenser; but if we did, we should never get back to Shakespeare in this book. The links, however, are there, and the chain is a strong one.[1] From the psychological point of view, Usk's *Testament of Love*, c. 1380, is of particular interest. In discussing it, C. S. Lewis[2] writes:

> Usk treats courtly love as a symbol of divine love; but, for that reason, he does not cease to treat courtly love. It is a mischievous error to suppose that in an allegory the author is "really" talking about the thing symbolized, and not at all about the thing that symbolizes; the very essence of the art is to talk about both.

I think we might well bear this thought in mind when considering the Shakespearean heroine—other characters, for the present, I leave aside: I suggest she has life and meaning at two levels, and Shakespeare is writing about both. If that should prove to be true, we need feel no surprise. Centuries of European tradition lie behind the creating of such figures—and also, perhaps, a disposition of the unconscious mind. But there is one element in Shakespeare's heroines that is not to be found in the Rose: it is the Platonic conception of Beauty, which the Middle Ages had forgotten, and which the Renaissance translators revived.

[1] See C. S. Lewis, *The Allegory of Love*.
[2] *Ibid.*, p. 225.

Chapter IV

"THE TWO GENTLEMEN OF VERONA"

IN *Love's Labour's Lost* Shakespeare took two activities, learning and loving; first, he displayed them, in superficial forms, as antagonistic; then, by deepening and expanding the meaning of each, he drew them together: at the end, the characters embark on a fresh course of study, which will be crowned by love. Out of jarring elements, a new unity has been created. This applies both to the outer world and to the inner; but since the process is initiated within, the play finally points to a fuller discovery, or expansion, of the self. For Shakespeare, this is certainly a conscious aim. He never loses it. And we may follow him, stage by stage, on a spiritual adventure. This voyage of discovery evidently seemed of great importance to him; because, as many instances will show, he was prepared, when necessary, to sacrifice theatrical effect to his philosophic purpose.

In *The Two Gentlemen of Verona* he takes two qualities—this time, friendship and love. He exhibits them in opposition:

> —In love
> Who respects friend? V. iv

And then, acting on principles that we will presently discuss, he resolves the conflict into the harmony of a new whole, ending with the climatic line:

> One feast, one house, one mutual happiness. V. iv

Clearly, he is using the same method in both plays, and it is one he will not forget:

> —I would by contraries
> Execute all things— *T.* II. i

that is, by bringing the contraries into a creative relationship all problems may be solved. From play to play, we shall watch the sphere of the self, or of self-knowledge, being expanded; and in time we shall be brought, with understanding, to the proposition that to be true to oneself makes all falsity impossible. It is to this state of truth or constancy to the self and to love that Shakespeare is leading his characters. In this play, we have the line:

> O heaven, were man
> But constant, he were perfect! V. iv

The idea is reiterated many times; and Shakespeare implies that when this condition is achieved, it will be reflected in the world. Cosmos is emergent from chaos first within and then without.

*   *   *

The play opens with two young men, bosom friends from childhood, who, for the first time in their lives, are about to part. Valentine is to set out for Milan, the purpose of his journey is to see the world: Proteus is to stay in Verona, because he will not leave his sweetheart. Valentine's first speech to him is somewhat lofty:

> Home-keeping youth have ever homely wits . . .
> I rather would entreat thy company
> To see the wonders of the world abroad,

Than, living dully sluggardized at home,
Wear out thy youth with shapeless idleness.
But since thou lovest—   I. i

Proteus is in love with Julia. It turns out to be an
unreliable sort of love—although not irredeemable—
that fails at the first temptation. Valentine, who has
never been in love, is even more condescending on this,
in fact, he is scornful:

If haply won, perhaps a hapless gain;
If lost, why then a grievous labour won . . .
. . . by love the young and tender wit
Is turn'd to folly . . .
But wherefore waste I time to counsel thee . . . ?
                                                         I. i

We at once suspect, remembering *Love's Labour's
Lost*, that the supercilious Valentine is about to be
educated, that love will be the subject of his studies, and
that at the end of the play Shakespeare will touch a
deeper level than we expect in what Quiller-Couch has
called "a light and jocund Italianate comedy". That
these guesses prove correct encourages confidence in
the reliability of Shakespearean patterns. Here, once
again, the false is to be contrasted with, and stripped
from the true; and henceforth we should expect this
from Shakespeare. He is always sensitive to the fact
that every virtue has a corresponding falsity, masquerad-
ing under the same name; and we should constantly
remind ourselves that when his characters speak of
"love", "honour", "nobility", and so forth, we must
measure their conceptions by his standard if we are to
discover what he really intends. False Semblant is very

cunning. To rely on habitual reactions will never do. And Shakespeare's own judgments do not rest on the conventional compromises, but on constancy to principles, by no means obvious, that we must try to ascertain.

We will follow the thread of Valentine's character first.

When he and Proteus part, Valentine is of the opinion that love is folly, "one fading moment" bought at a ridiculous price; and by implication, he rates his love-lorn friend a fool. When they meet again, in the second act, this time at Milan, Valentine's education has begun. He has fallen in love with Silvia. And he now candidly admits that it was he who was the fool:

> O gentle Proteus, love's a mighty lord,
> And hath so humbled me, as I confess
> There is no woe to his correction,
> Nor to his service no such joy on earth. II. iv

This is progress, these are the proper sentiments. And we may notice that the full list of symptoms that Valentine here records of himself, as well as the seven signs that his servant Speed ludicrously describes, are all contained, or have close correspondences, in the discourse of the god of love in *The Romance of the Rose*. But Valentine has by no means reached the goal that Shakespeare intends. And it is soon clear that he is passing through the same phases with which we have already been made familiar in *Love's Labour's Lost*. Glancing back, we may recall that there were four: scoffing—"A woman that is like a German clock!"; sonnetry and idolatry—"that makes flesh a divinity";

deception—"Love doth approach disguised"; and penance, a period of banishment to the "naked hermitage", after which, the Rose is won. But in Shakespeare, the promised fulfilment has something mystical and mysterious about it—increasingly so in later plays—quite unlike the conclusion of Jean de Meun.

Valentine, in the second act, is now in the sonnetry and idolatry class, a most promising pupil. "Call her divine!" he orders Proteus. And the highest honour he can invent for any other woman is:

> To bear my lady's train, lest the base earth
> Should from her vesture chance to steal a kiss,
> And, of so great a favour growing proud,
> Disdain to root the summer-swelling flower,
> And make rough winter everlastingly.

To which Proteus very justly answers:

> Why, Valentine, what braggardism is this?   II. iv

But by Shakespeare's measure, Valentine is doing well; he is passing through a phase in which truth is compounded with nonsense; this is normal, and what matters is that he is nearer to truth now than he was in the previous act. But Shakespeare brings his characters to self-knowledge by putting them through a number of tests, and Valentine is about to be tested.

*   *   *

The Duke of Milan is Valentine's host and Silvia's father. He is an indispensable figure in their love-affair—but he forbids it: he favours Valentine's rival, Thurio. Sylvia loves Valentine and hates Thurio.

We are in no doubt that the duke's attitude is wrong; but is Valentine therefore right to deceive a generous host and attempt to abduct his daughter? We will notice later how frequently in Shakespeare it is the duty of children to rebel, in the right way, against their parents: quite often, the older generation represents the old law, which must be superseded by the new. But laudable rebellion is a fine art, and it does not extend to elaborate deception and a multitude of lies.

Valentine's situation here, and his remedy, closely resemble those of the lover in *The Romance of the Rose*. We remember that Bialacoil, the lady's gracious self, was imprisoned by her suspicious guardians in a tower. This is what the duke now does to Silvia:

> I nightly lodge her in an upper tower,
> The key whereof myself have ever kept:
> And thence she cannot be conveyed away.
>
> III. i

In the *Romance*, the first step in the solution of this problem was to enlist the services of False Semblant, who even suggests—but the passage is not in Chaucer's translation—the use of a rope-ladder. Valentine also employs False Semblant; and this must be accounted a fault in him, leading directly to the penance of banishment.

The enlistment of False Semblant in the service of love has a literary background, as we have noticed, which is relevant at this point. Guillaume de Lorris would not have countenanced such a sin; it is Jean de Meun who makes the god of love accept False Semblant. This is one of Jean's many heresies. And because

Chaucer translated these treasonable passages, he was, he tells us, severely reprimanded by Love:

> And of myn olde servaunts thou misseyest,
> And hindrest hem, with thy translacioun . . .
> Thou mayst hit nat denye;
> For in pleyn text, with-outen nede of glose,
> Thou hast translated the Romaunce of the Rose,
> That is an heresye ageyns my lawe—[1]

For this fault, Chaucer had to do a penance—which was to write in love's honour *The Legend of Good Women*. Shakespeare also requires a penance. When the lover resorts to False Semblant, whose masks and shapes are manifold, he must pay for it. But the Shakespearean penance does more than wash away his sin: it gives him a new insight, by which he will be able to distinguish between the appearance of love and love's reality.

Valentine, betrayed by Proteus, is caught red-handed, rope-ladder and all. He is therefore banished by the duke:

> Why, Phaeton—for thou art Merops' son!—
> Wilt thou aspire to guide the heavenly car,
> And with thy daring folly burn the world?
> Wilt thou reach stars, because they shine on thee?
> Go base intruder, over-weening slave,
> Bestow thy fawning smiles on equal mates.
>
> III. i

But what really has to be banished, and will be, is the presence of False Semblant in Valentine himself; and of this, self-deception forms an important part. The effect of the duke's sentence is therefore salutary. And

---

[1] *The Legend of Good Women*, Prologue, Text B, lines 323-330.

the shock of it immediately increases Valentine's understanding of the true nature of love. I have suggested that the heroine, according to Shakespeare's habitual allegory, is a love-symbol; and being so, she must of necessity coincide with a quality within the hero. More than to anything else, it is to this quality—love, as a standard in his own soul—that the hero must be constant. If he is not—as I have tried to show in discussing Shakespeare's tragedies—he is lost. But he cannot be constant, understandingly, until he has realized love as a divine essence within. And Shakespeare uses his heroines to show us, in allegory the making of this discovery: he does so here, and he is still doing it, to take a single example, in *The Winter's Tale*, where Florizel says:

—I cannot be
Mine own, or anything to any, if
I be not thine—   *W.T.* IV. iii

This is a most important principle in Shakespeare; and in the soliloquy that follows Valentine's sentence of banishment, we see it clearly for the first time. Henceforth, if we bear this idea in mind, it will shed light on many an obscure situation. Valentine exclaims:

—Silvia is myself: banished from her,
Is self from self . . .
She is my essence: and I leave to be,
If I be not by her fair influence
Fostered, illumined, cherished, kept alive.

III. i

It would seem to be Shakespeare's proposition here that love is the soul's essence, so that when it denies love, it denies its own being. And since his method is to show the hero making a gradual discovery of love and beauty—through the shadows to the reality—it is likely that he is thinking in terms of the Platonic ascent.

Although the vast subject of renaissance Neo-Platonism is beyond the scope of this book, some mention of it cannot be avoided here. Plato initiated the theory that love in its desire for the beautiful will lead the soul, at last, to the eternal Beauty. The Neo-Platonists affirmed the identity of the Good, the Beautiful and the Divine. And in the fifteenth century, Marsilio Ficino, who did more than anyone else to promote the Platonic revival of the Renaissance, Christianized this body of ideas. He did so with signal success; but although he was himself in holy orders, he was not always orthodox, and notably on one important point: he follows Plato and Plotinus in insisting that the soul is intrinsically divine. "You must question the pious mind," he writes, "presenting to it the soul pure as you received it, not enslaved by the body nor soiled with the taint of vices. The mind will then answer that the soul is not only incorporeal but also divine."[1] This was by no means an isolated opinion. It was supported by a great tradition. And if we set the Shakespearean hero and heroine against this background, it is not difficult to understand why they should be one in self and essence, and yet be unaware of it, until their mutual love, not satisfied with less than complete union, has led them to the revelation of the spiritual beauty in themselves.

[1] *Theologia Platonica*, Book I, chapter ii.

Expressed in terms of romance, this is substantially the position that the Florentine Platonists had already established in the language of religion and philosophy. Writing of love and friendship, Ficino had said: "A true and stable union between several persons cannot be established except through the eternal unity itself. But the true and eternal unity is God Himself."[1] It was Ficino's wish that the members of the Florentine Academy should be united in this ideal manner, which amounted to the principle that perfect love, perfect self-knowledge, and mystical union with God are the same.

That Shakespeare was acquainted with the current forms of Neo-Platonism is indubitable, it is probable that he knew a fair amount of pure Platonism as well, and it is being increasingly recognized that there is allegory in his plays. We must expect, then, that part of the allegory will yield to a Neo-platonic interpretation, although there are many other elements in it as well.

*   *   *

The opening scene of the fourth act is a highway running through a forest. Outlaws are lying in ambush. The banished Valentine, with his servant Speed, comes along the road, and the outlaws spring upon them. There is a brief parley. And it is soon evident that these outlaws are not the common robbers we expect:

> Know, then, that some of us are gentlemen,
> Such as the fury of ungoverned youth
> Thrust from the company of awful men.   IV. i

---

[1] *Collected Works*, Basel, 1561, page 777.

And after a few more words, they make Valentine—
a chance wayfarer entirely unknown to them—an
astonishing offer:

> —be the captain of us all:
> We'll do thee homage and be ruled by thee,
> Love thee as our commander and our king.

But if not:

> —thou diest!

If we have a feeling for Shakespearean allegory,
everything about this scene—which is quite unrealistic,
but highly symbolic—suggests that there is a meaning
below the surface.

Kingship or death: it is the alternative, in respect of
the soul's inner kingdom, that Shakespeare unfailingly
presents to us in his major plays. What the tragic hero
does, as he yields to a series of temptations, is to lose,
step by step, the lordship of his own soul:

> —and the state of man,
> Like to a little kingdom, suffers then
> The nature of an insurrection.   *J.C.* II. i

In this condition of inner turmoil, self-sovereignty is
replaced by the fury of ungoverned passions; and the
outcome, as Shakespeare invariably depicts it, is
tragedy and death. Conversely, to enter the Shakespearean path of regeneration, the hero must gain
command of himself. All Shakespearean drama is
concerned with this, to him, fundamental problem of
self-sovereignty. Those who achieve it—like the Duke
of Vienna and Prospero—become, for that reason,
something more than men. The circumstances under
which, little by little, it is either won or lost are of

perennial interest to him; and he presents them on the stage allegorically. Sometimes he speaks *in propria persona*:

> Poor soul, the centre of my sinful earth,
> Fool'd by these rebel powers that thee array—
>
> *S.* 146

And occasionally, as in Richard II's soliloquy in the dungeon of Pomfret, it is made clear that the battle, the storm, the drama are all in the mind: there, in himself, Richard is deposed, and "king'd again". The phrase is akin to the saying in the Gospels that a man must be reborn; for in Shakespearean terms, the hero *must* be "king'd again". This places the alternative that is offered to Valentine—kingship or death—in a wide context of Shakespearean thought: in fact, it is a cardinal idea. And we may therefore suspect that Shakespeare is again using one of his favourite dramatic devices, the death-shock, as a preliminary to a deeper view of life.

If this scene is a parable—and I believe Shakespeare put many parables into his plays—then it would seem that the forest is another version of the "naked hermitage" of *Love's Labour's Lost*, or of "the life removed" of *Measure for Measure*, or of the chapel of penitence in which Leontes, as I have tried to show elsewhere,[1] learned how the tragic wound may be healed. Shakespeare never ran short of metaphors, but one clear conception is behind all these: a hero who is on the up-going path must, at some time, spend a period in the wilderness; and the purpose of doing so

---

[1] See *The Shakespearean Ethic,* chapter 11.

is to gain self-knowledge, self-sovereignty, and a fuller realization of love. It may come to him as a penance imposed, or as a decision of his own, but come it will. If he passes through it successfully, he will be well on the way to being "a perfect man". And this is a consummation which not only Shakespeare, but the men of the Renaissance in general thought about a great deal.

> Man is his own star; and the soul that can
> Render an honest and a perfect man,
> Commands all light, all influence, all fate;
> Nothing to him falls early or too late.
> Our acts our angels are, or good or ill,
> Our fatal shadows that walk by us still.[1]

The lines are by Beaumont and Fletcher, the inspiration of them may have been Shakespeare, but the ideal is of the age. Or perhaps we should say that the ideal is common to humanity, but at some periods it is given special stress, and that the Renaissance was one. However this may be, Shakespeare held very definite views on "the perfect man", and on the manner of his emergence from the chrysalis of *l'homme moyen sensuel*, the ordinary us. There is no reason to suppose that these ideas dawned on him only when he was at the apex of his powers; on the contrary, the evidence suggests that he held them, at least in outline, from the beginning, and that it is mainly his ability to impart them that improves.

If the forest does stand for the same conception as the "naked hermitage", then what of the outlaws, who spring upon the hero there? We notice, to begin with,

[1] *The Honest Man's Fortune*, epilogue.

that they are really gentlemen, and their background is much like Valentine's own. He assumes command of them, but remains constant in himself to his ideal of love. As a result of this the outlaws are pardoned at the end of the play, and all are restored, but still under Valentine's guidance, to their true estates. If this is a parable, then it is not very difficult to pierce. The outlaws must be the "rebel powers" that "array" the hero's soul. During his sojourn in the wilderness he has to face them, learn to know them for what they are, and control them. If he does not rule them, they will destroy him; but if he does, it will be for their salvation as well as his. For they are not presented to us as evils to be rooted out, but rather as true powers of the self which are either untamed, "as the fury of ungoverned youth", or have run wild. It would seem as if the first purpose of the hero's penance is to control this unregenerate nature, to chasten, purify and restore the "rebel powers". It is not an easy thing to accomplish, as, in soliloquy, Valentine laments:

> These are my mates, that make their wills their
>   law—
>   —I have much to do
> To keep them from uncivil outrages.   V. iv

This is, of course, a world-wide theme, and there is no religion in which some form of it does not appear. It is not original to Shakespeare, who is the prince of syncretists. But his constancy to these principles—as, I think, can be shown in play after play—does seem to me impressive: and they are the preliminary to his portrait of "the perfect man".

Something more than introspection and command is needed for Shakespearean perfection: the "crown and hearted throne" must be surrendered to Love. That is why, in the major plays, the hero's relations with the heroine, when she is an allegorical figure of love, are a measure of his spiritual rise or fall. However, the attendant circumstances may appear, when Hamlet insults Ophelia, we may be certain he is travelling down; and when Florizel affirms his constancy to Perdita, he is moving up. Valentine affords us a first, and inevitably an immature example of this principle applied. In the same soliloquy in which he tells of his struggle to keep his "mates" from uncivil outrage, he murmurs what is virtually a prayer:

> Repair me with thy presence, Silvia!   V. iv

And who is Silvia? All through, but particularly in this context, Silvia is a personification of Love or of the Platonic Beauty that is love's eternal goal. Valentine is passing, with success, something very like the test that, we may remember, was set to the King of Navarre:

> If frosts and fasts, hard lodging and thin weeds,
> Nip not the gaudy blossoms of your love,
> But that it bear this trial and last love,
> Then, at the expiration of the year,
> Come, challenge me, challenge me by these
>   deserts,
> And, by this virgin palm now kissing thine,
> I will be thine.   *L.L.L.* V. ii

Valentine is bearing a comparable trial and maintaining his love; and the reward is that his "prayer" is answered—Silvia joins him in the forest. If we may make an inference from the position Shakespeare takes up in later plays—in *Measure for Measure*, for example —then, having passed the test, Valentine ought to be, if not yet a perfect man, at least something above the ordinary. And in particular he ought to possess—on the analogy of the Duke of Vienna and Prospero—the power to make creative mercy effective. Perhaps, that is what Shakespeare is trying to demonstrate in the last scene. This *dénouement* has called forth a torrent of adverse criticism, and I think it likely that Shakespeare was the first person to recognize that it fails. But if our supposition is correct, that would be a minor matter: the significance would lie in the attempt. For the moment, however, we must leave Valentine in the forest. It is necessary to follow the career of Proteus before we consider what Quiller-Couch has called "the infamous finale".

*　　*　　*

Proteus is the first sketch of a type of character that is of the highest importance in Shakespeare: the erring hero, who would, if strict justice were done to him, come to a tragic end; but who is, in the event, saved by Shakespearean justice. Shakespearean justice, as it appears in the great plays of healing, where tragedy is resolved, is a quality inseparable from love, of which the purpose is not the punishing, but the saving of the offender. This shines as a steady light throughout Shakespeare, and in this play we watch it being kindled.

At the opening, as we have seen, Proteus and Valentine, life-long friends, part. Proteus, a "home-keeping youth", is held in Verona by an attachment that he supposes to be love. But it is worth noticing a remark that he lets fall, in the first scene:

I am not Love.

This may be one of those subtle hints that Shakespeare likes to give to the heedful listener, akin to Iago's, "I am not myself". We cannot feel sure that it is so, in such an early play; but when we have once established the special place of love and the self in Shakespeare's philosophy, and also noticed how fond he is of speaking *sotto voce* to those who have conditioned themselves to hear the remarks, then no speech of this kind can slip by unquestioned. And we may think back to it, when Valentine says of Silvia, who is certainly an allegorical figure of Love, "She is my essence". Love is not—or, at least, not yet—of the essence in Proteus. His is a counterfeit of the real thing. But the love of his sweetheart, Julia, is true: and it is Shakespeare's contention that there is an alchemical power in this that may transmute the counterfeit to gold.

Valentine has hardly left Verona when Proteus, most unwillingly, is also uprooted. His father ordains that he must travel:

> I have consider'd well his loss of time,
> And how he cannot be a perfect man,
> Not being tried and tutor'd in the world.
>
> I. iii

Once again, we have the theme of the "perfect man". And again it is made clear that perfection is not gained by being sheltered from temptation. *Constancy* is a key-word in this connection: we hear much of it in this play; and in *Measure for Measure* it is among the points made by the duke. Ultimately, the triumphing hero is seen to be constant to the highest quality in himself— "to thine own self be true"; and correctly understood, that is the only thing that is needful. Shakespeare, as has been said, conceives this highest quality as love, symbolizes it by the heroine, and we may gauge the hero's progress by his relations with her. Inconstancy to the ideal is, therefore, the all-inclusive sin—"were man but constant, he were perfect".

Naturally, this is a matter of degree. The ripening of virtue requires time, and Proteus is young. In the melancholy hour, when he must part from Julia, he exclaims:

O, how this spring of love resembleth
The uncertain glory of an April day,
Which now shows all the beauty of the sun,
And by and by a cloud takes all away!   I. iii

In spite of the disgraceful treachery that is to come, it is evident that we are intended to look on Proteus as kindly as we can. He turns out to be a young knave, but he is not a hardened villain; and his faults are mainly to be attributed to the uncertain weather of spring. That is the mood Shakespeare wishes to evoke. In point of fact, the later behaviour of Proteus is so caddish that it is difficult to feel indulgent. But I am only concerned with trying to establish what Shakespeare aimed at; to estimate the extent of his success in making the audience appreciate these aims is a different matter.

Proteus, then, is shipped off to Milan—"shipped" quite literally, an oddity I will not attempt to explain!—

and when he gets there, Valentine introduces him to Silvia. In later work, Shakespeare would have presented this as a temptation scene; but that is a technique he has not yet developed. It is a test, none the less; and Proteus fails it completely. At sight of Silvia, Julia is forgotten; and he is infatuated by the true sweetheart of his best friend. He imparts this to us in two soliloquys: interesting prefigurements of the revelations of inner conflict that Shakespeare gives us, after temptation scenes, in his major plays:

> Methinks my zeal to Valentine is cold,
> And that I love him not as I was wont.
> O, but I love his lady too too much!
> And that's the reason I love him so little.
> How shall I dote on her with more advice,
> That thus without advice begin to love her!
> 'Tis but her picture I have yet beheld,
> And that has dazzled my reason's light—
>
> II. iv

This touches again on the appearance-and-reality theme of *Love's Labour's Lost*, where clear sight was said to be lost by fixing the eye on the wrong object:

> As, painfully to pour upon a book
> To seek the light of truth . . .
> Your light grows dark by losing of your eyes.
>
> *L.L.L.* I. i

Now it is said to be a picture that dazzles "reason's light". Book and picture are metaphors for what seems, but is not truth. Before long we shall find Proteus doting on Silvia's picture literally. Like the lords who wooed the masked ladies by their favours—"taking

the sign for she"—he knows Love only "by the jewel
on her sleve". But to mistake the shadow for the
substance is the downfall of all Shakespeare's tragic
heroes, and accordingly, in his next soliloquy, we find
Proteus much nearer to the gulf:

> To leave my Julia, shall I be forsworn;
> To love fair Silvia, shall I be forsworn;
> To wrong my friend, I shall be much forsworn;
> And even that power, which gave me first my oath,
> Provokes me to this threefold perjury.
>
> .   .   .   .   .
>
> I will forget that Julia is alive,
> Remembering that my love to her is dead;
> I cannot now prove constant to myself,
> Without some treachery used to Valentine.
>
> II. vi

We witness, here, the birth of Shakespeare's design for
tragedy. Proteus is about to betray his best friend—
and much more. If we look ahead, we may observe
that Duncan was Macbeth's king, Brutus "was
Caesar's angel", Desdemona was Othello's faithful
wife, Perdita was Leontes' true child—one after
another, these protagonists kill the best thing in their
own lives. In this, Shakespeare is linking them
deliberately with Judas, "with him that did betray the
Best". And in the last analysis, Shakespeare interprets
this subjectively: they are betraying themselves, that
divine immanence on which rests the possibility of their
perfection, the reality they lose for the illusion.

If Shakespeare had been writing in one of the savage
moods of his maturity, he might easily have drawn

Proteus as a monster. Proteus betrays Valentine, cheats Thurio, deceives the duke, and does his best to seduce Silvia. How is it that he is not lost? There is a compound answer to this, and the part Valentine plays in it will be discussed when we come to the last scene; but the aspect of it that is shown to us first, exemplifies a principle that is constant to all Shakespearean salvation: the counteraction of Love. Just as, in *Measure for Measure*, the pleading of Mariana, Angelo's discarded sweetheart, is decisive in winning his reprieve from death, so now does Julia, the rejected, come to serve Proteus in disguise. In the *Romance of the Rose*, as we noticed, it is made plain that love is superior to justice.[1] Shakespeare, with his extraordinary gift of weaving diverse threads into a single pattern, presents love-justice as a unity. Julia's constant love, and Valentine's "perfect" justice, work, though in appearance separately, in absolute accord.

*　　*　　*

We must now see how the scene in Milan is set for the coming of Julia. Proteus tells the duke of Valentine's plan of elopement; and as, in *The Romance of the Rose*, the lover is turned out of the garden and Bialacoil shut up in the tower, so it is with Valentine and Silvia. False Semblant, now personified, is left to cheat everybody. Proteus plans to gain access to Silvia by offering assistance to her asinine suitor, Thurio, whom the duke perversely desires for a son-in-law. It is a nasty piece of trickery, which includes the slandering of Valentine;

---

[1] See above, page 93.

but we may give Proteus credit for showing a welcome sense of humour at this point. When Thurio takes a dim view of his chances, Proteus revives his hope and gives advice:

> As much as I can do, I will effect:
> But you, Sir Thurio, are not sharp enough;
> You must lay lime to tangle her desires
> By wailful sonnets . . .
> Say that upon the altar of her beauty
> You sacrifice your tears, your sighs, your heart:
> Write till your ink be dry, and with your tears
> Moist it again . . .
> After your dire-lamenting elegies,
> Visit by night your lady's chamber-window
> With some sweet consort; to their instruments
> Tune a deploring dump . . .
> This, or else nothing, will inherit her.

Nothing will. But Thurio, a clown in court clothing, is delighted with the idea, and rushes off to engage musicians, with the remark:

> I have a sonnet that will serve the turn.   III. ii

His no-doubt-delectable lines are not made known to us. But we do have the musicians, the mandolins and the moonlit serenade; and with them, one of Shakespeare's lovely songs: Who is Silvia?

It is at this point that Julia steps into the fourth act— always, we may remember, the love-act; and when Shakespeare puts music, two heroines and moonlight on to the stage at once, we may be quite certain that the power of love is about to change discords into heavenly harmony. It may not succeed immediately, but the transmutation has begun.

> Who is Silvia? What is she,
>   That all our swains commend her?
> Holy, fair, and wise is she;
>   The heaven such grace did lend her—
>
> IV. ii

Perhaps Shakespeare is seeing Silvia as Beauty at this point—the Platonic Beauty in the sense in which the Renaissance had re-interpreted the idea—while Julia is Love. If so, they are essentially one; and certainly, from their first meeting, we find them in accord.

We must glance back, for a moment, to the scene in the second act, where Julia plans this journey, with the help of her maid. It is in the source story. Shakespeare did not invent it, but he has deepened the idea in a way that is unmistakably his own. The reason Julia gives is simply "the inly touch of love": she cannot bear to be parted from her sweetheart any longer. Theatrically, we might take it as romantic caprice: realistically, for a girl to dress up as a boy and wander across Italy in search of her lover would be a scandal. Shakespeare is aware of both, but in his hands it is neither. He gets some fun out of the page's outfit, and, "What fashion, madam, shall I make your breeches?" But beneath the ripples, there is a deeper current running. Julia, in her first speech, asks her maid's advice:

> How, with my honour, I may undertake
> A journey to my loving Proteus.   II. vii

Lucetta is not encouraging. She observes that the way will be wearisome and long. To which Julia answers:

> A true-devoted pilgrim is not weary
> To measure kingdoms with his feeble steps;
> Much less shall she that hath Love's wings to
>   fly—

Lucetta still tries to dissuade. And Julia, though she might simply have given orders, seems rather to plead for approval, and concludes an enchanting speech with the lines:

> Then let me go, and hinder not my course:
> I'll be as patient as a gentle stream,
> And make a pastime of each weary step,
> Till the last step have brought me to my love;
> And there I'll rest, as after much turmoil
> A blessed soul doth in Elysium.

This is not a capricious or a wanton love; it is love as a pilgrim, love that will serve and suffer, and reach a perfect goal. Julia does not know she is on a mission of rescue; but Shakespeare is presenting a parable of love as a saving power.

Julia is naturally expecting to be welcomed by her lover: instead, at her first sight of him—herself standing in the shadows—she finds him serenading Silvia. Ostensibly, this is on Thurio's behalf; but the inn-keeper, who has brought Julia to the spot, soon informs her of his infatuation. She does not disclose herself, but reveals her bitterness in several asides. It is a hard test of love, and worse will follow.

There is, however, one good portent: Silvia does not wish to be a rival. When Thurio and the musicians

have gone, Silvia, from her tower-window, speaks to
Proteus:

> —my will is even this:
> That presently you hie you home to bed.
> Thou subtle, perjured, false, disloyal man!
>
> . . . . .
>
> Return, return, and make thy love amends.
> For me, by this pale queen of night I swear,
> I am so far from granting thy request,
> That I despise thee for thy wrongful suit—

The two heroines, although they do not know each
other, are made allies by their constancy to love's ideal.
But Proteus is unabashed, and begs Sylvia for her
portrait:

> Vouchsafe me yet your picture for my love,
> The picture that is hanging in your chamber;
> To that I'll speak, to that I'll sigh and weep:
> For since the substance of your perfect self
> Is else devoted, I am but a shadow;
> And to your shadow will I make true love.

Sylvia—for no other valid reason than to enable Shakespeare to enrich his allegory—consents:

> I am very loath to be your idol, sir;
> But since your falsehood shall become you well
> To worship shadows and adore false shapes,
> Send to me in the morning, and I'll send it.
>
> IV. ii

The theme of shadow-worship is one that is never done
with in Shakespeare. No play is quite without it. He
handles it lightly and tragically, in laughter and in
despair; it is the foible of Armado, and the doom of
Macbeth. His tragic heroes pay lip-service to spirit and
truth, but they have lost consciousness of both; they

adore false shapes, not dreaming that they are false, and that is their disaster.

One advantage of studying the early plays is that we see such themes put simply. "Your picture for my love" set in contrast to "the substance of your perfect self" is a ransparent metaphor; it prepares us for the antithesis of the crown that is on the head and the crown in the heart; and that, in turn, leads to the subjective ideal of being "king'd again", and, at last, to an apocalypse of spiritual kingship: the kingdom of heaven is within. On the other hand, Silvia's lines carry us back to the love-in-disguise scenes of *Love's Labour's Lost,* and in particular to Rosaline's remark to the king:

> O vain petitioner! beg a greater matter;
> Thou now request'st but moonshine in the water.
> V. ii

When Proteus is worshipping the portrait, that is very much what he has—"moonshine in the water". But the same will be true of Macbeth, making another Golgotha to win a metal crown. Part of the secret of the regenerating heroes is that they "beg a greater matter". But to do so, they must have clear sight. And the relentless stripping away of the trappings and the suits, which continues in parable and allegory from play to play, is all to this purpose, "Know thyself!"

Julia takes up the cross of love in this scene. And her closing words are of sorrow, not defeat:

> —it hath been the longest night
> That e'er I watched, and the most heaviest.
> IV. ii

*   *   *

From the realistic point of view it is, of course, absurd that a man should engage his one-time sweetheart as a page, keep her in close attendance on him, and never notice who she was. But a painful testing of constancy in service is one part of Shakespeare's parable, and the love-blindness of Proteus is another part; so Proteus takes Julia into his employment. Her first duty is to act as a go-between in his affair with Silvia, and she murmurs an aside:

> Alas, poor Proteus! thou hast entertain'd
> A fox to be the shepherd of thy lambs.
> Alas, poor fool! why do I pity him
>
> . . . . .
>
> Because I love him, I must pity him.　　IV. iv

He tells her to take the selfsame ring that she gave to him on parting, and present it with his compliments to her rival. And she is to bring back the portrait. Silvia gives her the portrait, and a message:

> Go give your master this: tell him, from me,
> One Julia, that his changing thoughts forget,
> Would better fit his chamber than this shadow.

But the ring she refuses to accept:

> The more shame for him that he sends it me;
> For I have heard him say a thousand times
> His Julia gave it him at his departure.
> Though his false finger have profaned the ring,
> Mine shall not do his Julia so much wrong.
>
> 　　　　　　　　　　　　　　　　IV. iv

The two heroines are therefore in complete accord.

And in her soliloquy that closes the act, Julia says, as she picks up Silvia's portrait:

> Come, shadow, come, and take this shadow up,
> For 'tis thy rival.

This is a most important clue to the meaning of the last scene of the play. Rivalry exists only between the shadows: unity resides in the reality behind them. In their inner nature, there is no division between Silvia and Julia. And Julia's soliloquy goes on:

> O thou senseless form,
> Thou shalt be worshipp'd, kiss'd, loved and
>   adored!
> And, were there sense in his idolatry,
> My substance should be statue in thy stead.
>
> IV. iv

This is precisely what Silvia has said already. Therefore we shall not end among the dangers of the eternal triangle, but in the stability of an ideal square.

In many respects, Shakespeare is sublimely careless: if some tangle of fact, which may seem important to his commentators, bores him, he seldom bothers to undo the knot; on the other hand, in niceties of allegory he is often meticulous. If Julia mentions that she played the part of Ariadne in a Pentecostal pageant, it is not padding (no more than Perdita's costume of Flora), it is a signpost to Julia's deeper significance. In fact, this confirms what we have already found reason to think of her: she is the thread of love, leading from the labyrinth, she is cruelly misused, but she will win her crown of stars. Her story is a parable of love that suffers, saves, and sheds a light from heaven. We may

125

think that, in point of fact, Julia does not effect very much; but when we examine the conclusion, we shall find that her constancy was indispensable.

*　　*　　*

Before turning to the last act, we must give a glance at the minor characters. Proteus and Valentine are each attended by a comic servant—Launce and Speed respectively. And Launce is a servant to his own ungrateful servant, Crab. In *Love's Labour's Lost* we found that the sub-plot—the progress of Armado's love-affair with Jaquenetta—paralleled the main theme, at a lower level, as if to underline it; and naturally we wonder if the same device is to be found here. If so, if the allegories of the over- and the under-plots again turn out to have the same meaning, we have an excellent check upon interpretation.

When Launce and Speed are discussing their masters, and in particular, whether the projected marriage between Proteus and Julia will take place, we have this dialogue:

LAUNCE: Ask my dog: if he say ay, it will; if he say no, it will; if he shake his tail and say nothing, it will.

SPEED: The conclusion is, then, that it will.

LAUNCE: Thou shalt never get such a secret from me but by a parable.

SPEED: 'Tis well that I get it so.　　　　　II. v

From this we might risk a guess that the parable is about Proteus and Julia; that there is a dog in it; and that if the secret is not too deep for Speed, we, too, should be able to unearth it. It is also clear that we are being invited to look to the dog.

126

The dog makes his first appearance in the scene where Launce, who has to accompany his master to Milan, is lamenting the break-up of his family-life:

> Nay, 'twill be this hour ere I have done weeping; all the kind of the Launces have this very fault. I have received my proportion, like the prodigious son, and am going with Sir Proteus to the Imperial's court. I think Crab, my dog, be the sourest-natured dog that lives: my mother weeping, my father wailing, my sister crying, our maid howling, our cat wringing her hands, and all our house in a great perplexity, yet did not this cruel-hearted cur shed one tear: he is a stone, a very pebble stone—

Then follows a rich scene of clowning, in which Launce re-enacts the leave-taking, with the members of his family represented by some very old shoes, apparently beyond repair. At the end of this woeful performance, the complaint against Crab is repeated:

> Now the dog all this while sheds not a tear, nor speaks a word; but see how I lay the dust with my tears. II. iii

When Crab gets to Milan, his character does not improve: in fact, court-life seems to bring out the worst in him. Although continuing ungrieved himself, he becomes a cause of grief to others, as Launce explains:

> When a man's servant shall play the cur with him, look you, it goes hard: one that I brought up of a puppy; one that I saved from drowning, when three or four of his blind brothers and sisters went to it! I have taught him, even as one would say precisely, "thus I would teach a dog". I was sent to deliver

him as a present to Mistress Silvia from my master; and I came no sooner into the dining-chamber, but he steps me to her trencher, and steals her capon's leg: O, 'tis a foul thing when a cur cannot keep himself in all companies! I would have, as one should say, one that takes upon him to be a dog indeed, to be, as it were, a dog at all things. If I had not had more wit than he, to take a fault upon me that he did, I think verily he had been hanged for't; sure as I live, he had suffered for't: you shall judge. He thrusts me himself into the company of three or four gentlemanlike dogs, under the duke's table: he had not been there—bless the mark—a pissing while, but all the chamber smelt him. "Out with the dog!" says one. "What cur is that?" says another. "Whip him out," says the third. "Hang him up," says the duke. I, having been acquainted with the smell before, knew it was Crab, and goes me to the fellow that whips the dogs: "Friend," quoth I, "you mean to whip the dog?" "Ay, marry, do I," quoth he. "You do him the more wrong," quoth I; " 'twas I did the thing you wot of." He makes me no more ado, but whips me out of the chamber. How many masters would do this for his servant? Nay, I'll be sworn, I have sat in the stocks for puddings he hath stolen, otherwise he had been executed; I have stood on the pillory for geese he hath killed, otherwise he had suffered for't. Thou thinkest not of this now. Nay, I remember the trick you served me when I took my leave of Madam Silvia: did not I bid thee still mark me, and do as I do? When didst thou see me heave up my leg, and make water against a gentlewoman's farthingale?   IV. iv

The first of these Launce-and-Crab scenes—act two, scene three—comes directly after the parting of Proteus and Julia; in the second of them—act two,

scene five—the servants are discussing whether
Proteus and Julia will marry; and the third is immediately followed by the scene in which Proteus engages
Julia as his page. The parable hardly needs interpretation; but it is an excellent example of the care
with which Shakespeare can construct when he chooses,
that is, when the point at issue interests him.

Crab is little better than "ingrateful man"—and,
incidentally, most undoglike. His resemblance to
Proteus is remarkable. Proteus, too, in his present
phase, is being "a dog in all things"; he, too, has thrust
himself into the company of gentlemanlike dogs around
the duke's table, and misbehaved there; and he would
have stolen more from Silvia, had he been able, than a
capon's leg. "O, 'tis a foul thing when a cur cannot keep
himself in all companies!" But there must be something
about Crab and Proteus that is lovable and worth
saving; and saved they are, by the "charity that
suffereth long and is kind". There can be no further
doubt that Launce and Julia both exemplify this
quality, and Shakespeare proceeds to give us one of
those neat tie-ups that are most satisfying. In the next
scene, where Julia is told to take her own ring and
present it to Silvia, she remarks aside:

How many women would do such a message?

IV. iv

It exactly corresponds to what Launce had said a few
minutes earlier:

How many masters would do this for his servant?

But Shakespeare, in all his work, never falters in the

belief that the greatest in the kingdom is the servant of all—provided always that he serve for love.

An analysis of the constructional method employed here will help us to probe Shakespeare's meaning in other plays. We notice that the saving mission of Julia to Proteus is paralleled, on a lower level, by that of Launce to Crab, and, on a higher level, by the reference to Ariadne and Theseus; we can hardly doubt that the ethics of the New Testament are implied. This is the kind of thing that we must be on the look out for in Shakespeare. He takes what he believes to be a spiritual truth, and illustrates it by a series of parables at descending levels—from the Gospels and the Classics, to the lovers and the clown.

*   *   *

Critical opinion on the fifth act is nearly unanimous.

". . . we are left face to face with a mistake in art . . ."

". . . a flaw too unnatural to be charged upon Shakespeare . . ."

". . . this most crucial blunder."

". . . infamous finale . . ."

". . . a piece of theatre botchwork . . ."

Much more might be quoted, and in some of it there is an odd trace of venom. It has been claimed that the offending portions are non-Shakespearean; yet they would seem to be required by the ensuing action. Certainly, this act, which in the form we have it contains only a hundred and seventy-three lines, must have been rather brutally cut, perhaps for some particular production, and that may account for much, but not for everything to which exception has been taken. But this criticism, however justifiable it may be, is based on the assumption that convincing character- ization and a good *coup de théâtre* is Shakespeare's only aim. I hope I have convinced my readers that it is not. Shakespeare is writing an allegory as well as a play, neither is finished, and the conclusion must take account of both. I will not claim that this answers the objections, but only that it has been overlooked.

When drama is also allegory, compromise is inevitable: sometimes the one and sometimes the other will predominate. And when a scene in Shakespeare presents difficulties from the dramatic and psycho- logical standpoints, we may suspect at once that the parable is being given special stress. This may account, in the present play, for Valentine's captaincy of the outlaws; and the last misdeed of which Launce accuses Crab is, as realism, incredible. Perhaps it will help us with the conclusion; but even if it does not, it must still be borne in mind.

At the beginning of the act, Silvia escapes, in the hope of joining Valentine. She is pursued. And after various confusions in the forest, she falls into the hands of Proteus—still attended by his "page". As Silvia is not to be won by fair words, Proteus threatens rape, and at that moment Valentine steps out from the trees:

> Ruffian, let go that rude uncivil touch!
>
> V. iv

So far, so good. Weapons glint. The *coup de théâtre* is admirable. But what about the allegory? That requires a perfect ending, and the play has only a hundred and thirteen more lines to run. Shakespeare has undertaken to do a good deal; and before we blame him for failure it is fair to consider his problem. Julia set out for Elysium, and she is not to be disappointed. The saving power of constancy to love is to be demonstrated; and also, perhaps, that of creative mercy. Valentine is at least approaching the condition of being a "perfect man", and he must act accordingly. And hardest of all, love and friendship, in their ideal state, are to be shown as one. To do all of this in the space at his disposal is impossible, but Shakespeare attempts it—and in that lies the fascination of the scene. The first step is the repentance of Proteus:

> Forgive me, Valentine: if hearty sorrow
> Be a sufficient ransom for offence,
> I tender't here. I do as truly suffer
> As e'er I did commit.   V. iv

As it stands, it is perfunctory and unconvincing; but it is an abiding principle with Shakespeare that sorrow and suffering do ransom an offence, and later he works this out in detail—notably in *The Winter's Tale*. Valentine, being on the ascending path, *must* accept this: again, it is a Shakespearean principle. We may look ahead, right up to *The Tempest*, and still find it in the words of Prospero:

>   —they being penitent,
> The sole drift of my purpose doth extend
> Not a frown further.   *T.* V. i

Valentine does but announce this theme:

> Who by repentance is not satisfied
> Is not of heaven nor earth—   V. iv

Rejection of it, in Shakespeare, would indicate a hell-ward course. There may, also, be a presage of something more in Valentine's forgiveness—the power of creative mercy, but I will not press this point. So far, whether the act has been tampered with or not, its leading ideas are characteristically Shakespearean. But is this true of the couplet that has caused most of the trouble? Is there any inner necessity for Valentine to continue:

> And, that my love may appear plain and free,
> All that was mine in Silvia I give thee.   V. iv

"One's impulse, upon this declaration," writes Quiller-Couch, "is to remark that there are, by this time, *no* gentlemen in Verona." It may be. But we must counter the impulse first by observing that Montaigne, who was certainly a gentleman by the standards of the age, would have approved these sentiments in principle. We have already seen that Jean de Meun rated friendship as a higher form of love, and I have suggested that it is Shakespeare's intention to present them as a harmony. Of course, in this play, he failed to do so to the conviction of his audience; but the couplet, I believe, is related to the purpose. In later work, it is evident that he is aiming to make division grow together, not as a compromise, but perfectly. And that this thought was now in his mind, before he had the literary experience to make it comprehensible to anyone else, is suggested by the last lines of the play:

> —our day of marriage shall be yours;
> One feast, one house, on mutual happiness.

Harmony between the two heroines has already been

established, and, clearly, we are meant to picture Valentine and Proteus, Silvia and Julia enjoying a happiness quite out of the ordinary. It may be that our reason is confounded by the contemplation of it, and that on the way there our sensibilities have been shocked. But this only proves what we might have expected: Shakespeare, at this stage, was unable to give adequate expression to his immense ideas. It is not his intention merely to endorse a familiar romantic standard: he is seeking a new ethic, one that will be conducive and appropriate to another golden age. In this scene he is not contrasting friendship with love, as Jean de Meun does, nor evaluating one in terms of the other: he is uniting them. In his reason, or excuse for this, he goes deeper than Montaigne.

> "If a man urge me", writes Montaigne, discussing his own experience of friendship, "to tell wherefore I loved him, I feele it cannot be expressed, but by answering; Because it was he, because it was my selfe."[1]

Shakespeare adds something to this. He assumes that love is the essence of the self, and that perfect love is therefore a recognition, in this innermost sphere, of identity. He has already announced this theme in, "She is my essence." He returns to it in future plays; and in *The Phoenix and the Turtle*, carries it as far, perhaps, as language ever will:

> So they love'd, as love in twain
> Had the essence but in one;
> Two distincts, division none:
> Number there in love was slain.

[1] Montaigne: *The Essays*, I, xxvii (Florio's translation)

At this level, obviously, distinctions of sex are less than irrelevant—they do not exist; and some, at least, of the sex ambiguities in Shakespeare may be better understood if we bear this conception in mind.

Perhaps we may yet find an acceptable meaning in the words of Valentine:

> All that was mine in Silvia I give thee.

But again we must raise the question, Who is Silvia? And again I suggest that, in Shakespeare's mind, she is more than a girl in a play; she is also a symbol of the eternal Beauty. No man possesses that for himself alone. Valentine has won his part in it by merit: on Proteus, it is bestowed as friendship's perfect gift.

Chapter V

TERENCE ELABORATED

BEFORE considering *Romeo and Juliet* we must again bring Terence into the picture. My readers will have noticed that *The Two Gentlemen of Verona* has, in the main, a Terentian shape; but we must establish this fact more definitely. I apologize if to do so seems repetitious; but it is an important stepping-stone, and it is worth making sure that it is a firm one. The act-structure of *The Two Gentlemen of Verona* may be briefly analysed as follows:

Act I

Two young men, Valentine and Proteus, are friends. Valentine is about to set out on a journey to finish his education. Proteus will not go with him because he is in love with Julia. Love and friendship are pulling in different ways, but it can hardly be called a conflict.

Act II

Valentine goes to Milan, and there falls in love with Silvia. Proteus is compelled to follow him; and when he is introduced to Silvia, he is infatuated by her. He is ready to forget Julia and to deceive Valentine. The conflict is now clear; it is between infatuation on the one side, and true love and friendship on the other. Again, the real battleground is in the heart, or soul, of the characters.

136

Act III

Infatuation seems likely to win. Valentine is banished. Proteus has a clear field to seduce Silvia if he can.

Act IV

True love intervenes. Julia follows her false sweetheart to win him back. Silvia and Valentine pass the test of separation, and remain true to each other.

Act V

The constancy of three characters redeems the inconstancy of the fourth. All are united in perfect harmony. Again, a number of shallow feelings have been dismissed; and there is a strong suggestion that love and friendship, in the deepest sense, are one.

Strictly speaking, the first act does not quite conform with the Terentian rules; but the pattern as a whole clearly does so, and other resemblances to *Love's Labour's Lost* are marked. In both plays, Shakespeare is working up to a would-be perfect synthesis.

This is Terence—with a difference. We see that for Shakespeare, even in these comedies, the primary conflict is not between groups of people, but between emotions, or groups of emotions within people. This shift of emphasis from the outer world to the inner is of great importance. Shakespeare increasingly takes the view that the physical struggle merely reflects the psychological, which in later plays is most clearly revealed by the soliloquies. The battle, the victory, the defeat—all, in his deeper meaning, take place in the soul. The philosophical background of this is partly

Platonic, the character-analysis of *The Romance of the Rose* is an influence, but the dramatic expression of it derives from the tradition of the Morality Plays. In these, the forces of light and darkness fight in and for the soul; and salvation or perdition is the outcome.

To exhibit this, Shakespeare inserts a new constructional element in the Terentian plan—a series of temptations or tests; to pass these tests brings an enhancement of life, to fail in them is a movement towards death. With this structural addition, the form that Terence employed for light entertainment becomes able to carry weighty philosophic ideas. But it has lost nothing thereby of its ability to present trifles gracefully. And so it provides Shakespeare with an almost ideal construction—one that he may use to stage anything, from the opposing powers of heaven and hell to a flirtation and a lovers' tiff. The heart-beat is conflict, but it may be a storm in a tea-cup or a tempest of tragedy. Schematically, therefore, we might illustrate the method in purely general terms, as a game between White and Black.

WHITE	*versus*	BLACK

in light comedy

The side we hope will win	The side we hope will lose
Sympathy	Antipathy
Truth	Falsity

in tragedy and regeneration plays

Love	Hate
Life	Death
Heaven	Hell
Cosmos	Chaos

In the course of the game, each side plays many cards. But Black always plays its highest trump-card in the third act, and White in the fourth. These are moments which we must particularly watch; for the side that plays the better card then will win the game in the fifth act. If White wins, the end is harmony: this may be just a happy ending, or it may be a great victory for the spirit, which is what the outcome of *Measure for Measure* and *The Winter's Tale* really is. If Black wins, the end is death.

As White and Black represent forces rather than people, the characters may change sides in the course of the play. When they do, tremendous consequences follow. In the second act of *Measure for Measure*, for example, Isabella, pleading for Claudio's life, is playing for White. In the third act, she is won over to Black, and herself says to Claudio, "Die, perish!" This success is, in fact, Black's trump-card, played as always in the third act. Conversely, in *The Winter's Tale*, Leontes at first plays for Black, but after his repentance, for White. In *Romeo and Juliet*, to which we now come, this change of sides is momentous; and it fits perfectly into the Terentian construction.

Act I

We are presented with a clear issue: what is to be the outcome of the love between Romeo and Juliet? White represents the forces working towards union and life; Black stands for those of separation and death. The background of conflict is made clear to us, and our sympathies are engaged.

Act II

White plays several cards: the last is the secret marriage. Black also plays: Tybalt sends a written challenge to Romeo.

Act III

Dramatically changing sides, Romeo plays for Black, and kills Tybalt. This is Black's best card, and so far as the lovers' life on earth is concerned, it proves unbeatable.

Act IV

Juliet plays for White. With the help of Friar Laurence, she executes the desperate plan of feigned death.

Act V

Black wins, in the sense that Romeo and Juliet both die. White wins, in the sense that their families are reconciled. The implications of this two-faced ending must be further examined.

Did Shakespeare intend to leave us with an equivocation? The two earlier plays lead to a synthesis. Could a similar intention explain the ambiguity here? *Mors janua vitae.* He may mean that, under certain circumstances, death is the gate of life. In the last scene, Juliet's tomb is called a "lantern", and this might be a denial of victory to the grave. But this is questionable. We must try to find the answer to it, and to other problems in this play, step by step.

Chapter VI

"ROMEO AND JULIET"

WHEN we read Shakespeare's non-historical plays in the order in which he wrote them—as far as this is ascertainable—a thing that strikes us immediately about *Romeo and Juliet* is that for the first time Shakespeare is gripped by his story. He does not play with it: he matches its emotional impetus with his own. He follows his source—Brooke's poem, *The Tragicall Historye of Romeus and Juliet*—fairly closely, but increases its explosive power by compression. Our first feeling is that the tragedy of these lovers is like a ferment of new wine which bursts the old wine-skins and is lost. Detailed allegory, being a work of the intellect, is not favoured by this uprush of emotion. Nevertheless, the Shakespearean parable is there.

The fact that in this play Shakespeare takes so much from Brooke provokes a general question. Are Shakespeare's borrowings to be discounted from the point of view of parable and plot? Are we to say, "he took this detail from so-and-so, and therefore he must not be given credit for the thought"? Or, on the other hand, should we maintain that Shakespeare was selective in his appropriations; that he took from his sources only what would fit into his own pattern; and that because this new context gives a new, or enhanced significance to the old ideas, they must therefore be accounted Shakespearean?

Fine critics could be cited in support of either

contention. But if we were to press the first to logical finality, subtracting from Shakespeare every phrase and conception for which we could find a source, the outcome would be near disintegration. The plays would begin to look like rag-mats, stitched together out of innumerable pieces of ancient material. We are compelled to revolt against this grotesque conclusion. We know that poetry is not created in that way. But we cannot deny the borrowings; and if judgment is not to sink to the level of caprice, we must have some standard for assessing them.

Coleridge has been censured for giving *Shakespeare* the credit for showing Romeo "love-bewildered" by Rosaline before he meets Juliet. But the issue is not simple: Coleridge may be right. To depict the hero worshipping the mask, the picture, the shadow, the moon in water, before he unveils the reality is a part of the Shakespearean love-pattern; and if it had not been, or, at any rate, if it had conflicted with the pattern, we may reasonably suppose that Shakespeare would have rejected this element of Brooke's. By selecting it with deliberation, he makes it, from our standpoint, his own. Details that are used with allegorical consistency from play to play must, it seems to me, be treated as Shakespeare's, whatever their source. Shakespeare was not a maker of rag-mats. But sometimes we may conceive of him as a jeweller, re-setting old gems into his own design. When we find a consistency in principles, then the origin of the illustrations that support them is of secondary importance. Naturally, however, marked deviation from the source-story will merit special attention.

Shakespeare must have had a great determination to make people see, feel and understand the cause of the world's tragedy. Human life is never free from the threat of calamity. Why is this so? Can the curse be lifted? Shakespeare never ceased to wrestle with these problems, and to do his utmost to make his audience face and grasp what he believed to be the facts. At the end of his plays, in particular, this is so—for example, in *Hamlet*:

> —give order that these bodies
> High on a stage be placed to the view;
> And let me speak to the yet unknowing world
> How these things came about: so shall you hear
> Of carnal, bloody, and unnatural acts,
> Of accidental judgments, casual slaughters;
> Of deaths put on by cunning and forc'd cause,
> And, in the upshot, purposes mistook
> Fall'n on the inventors' heads—   V. ii

But the study of the disease held no morbid fascination for him, and he is not a whit less preoccupied with the remedy. After pointing to the plague-pit in *Titus Andronicus*, he invites us to consider his cure:

> O! let me teach you how to knit again
> This scatter'd corn into one mutual sheaf,
> These broken limbs again into one body—
> > V. iii

We may not believe that he could do so, but it is worth while to enquire what his proposals were. Indeed, he insists on it. In *Romeo and Juliet*, his first deep analysis of tragedy, he is asking the audience to do much more than pity these lovers; he is urging and demanding that it shall exert its intelligence as well:

> Where be these enemies?—Capulet! Montague!
> See what a scourge is laid upon your hate—
>
> V. iii

Shakespeare, according to his method, is making a closing demonstration, "Look at the corpses in front of you—your own son and daughter! Why are they dead? For God's sake think!" And he is requiring the audience to do the same—not merely to shudder at the scourge, but also to ponder the reasons for the reconciliation with which the play ends. Let us now turn to the prologue:

> Two households, both alike in dignity,
>   In fair Verona, where we lay our scene,
> From ancient grudge break to new mutiny,
>   Where civil blood makes civil hands unclean.
> From forth the fatal loins of these two foes
>   A pair of star-cross'd lovers take their life;
> Whose misadventured piteous overthrows
>   Do with their death bury their parents' strife.

There is to be much of love, here, as well as of hate; and Shakespeare is intending to give us a wide view of both.

At the rise of the curtain, they are shown to us in the shape of the stupid brute. The serving-men of the house of Capulet have straightforward intentions with regard to all Montagues: they will murder the men and ravish the maids—hate and "love" in indistinguishable simplicity. But in this first scene, it is not so much the brutality as the stupidity that Shakespeare seems to find insufferable. We are never told the origin of the quarrel between the Capulets and the Montagues. None of the servants has any valid reason for hating anybody. It is

144

just "the ancient grudge", purposely presented in terms general to humanity. If Shakespeare had laid bare the cause, he would doubtless have shown it to be as empty as the jealousy of Othello; and what he does present is senseless strife in which there are no winners. It is clear that he finds it an affront to human intelligence; so, when the Montague servants enter, we have the dialogue appropriate.

ABRAHAM: Do you bite your thumb at us, sir?
SAMPSON: I do bite my thumb, sir.
ABRAHAM: Do you bite your thumb at us, sir?
SAMPSON (*aside to Gregory*): Is the law of our side if I say ay?
GREGORY: No.
SAMPSON: No, sir, I do not bite my thumb at you, sir; but I bite my thumb, sir.

It is idiotic—but enough:

Draw, if you be men! Gregory, remember
thy swashing blow.   I. i

So another bout of swashing has started in Verona; and it is meant to insult our reason. One of Shakespeare's favourite devices is to show that vast consequences flow from seeming-nothing. And yet it is not from nothing. As I have pointed out elsewhere, he sees the outer life as a reflection of the inner: and who seeks for reasons must enquire within.

There is a lightning sketch, in the first scene, of a huge panorama from the grotesque to the divine. The fight is stopped, for a few moments, by Benvolio:

Part, fools!
Put up your swords; you know not what you do.
                                        I. i

We cannot miss the echo from the Gospels. This senseless hate—the principle of hate—is leading to the crucifixion of love. Whether Brooke thought of it or not, Shakespeare is holding that conception in his mind. In *The Two Gentlemen of Verona*, we have been introduced to the theme of the effectiveness of love's self-sacrifice: Julia suffered both for and from her faithless lover; and because she did so, they regained their mutual joy. Mariana does the same for Angelo in *Measure for Measure*—it is one of Shakespeare's fundamental ideas. We are led to it again, in a wider context, here. When the reconciled enemies stand together in the last scene, their final reflection is not so much on the death as on the worth of Romeo and Juliet. Montague says:

> For I will raise her statue in pure gold;
> That whiles Verona by that name is known,
> There shall no figure at such rate be set
> As that of true and faithful Juliet.

And Capulet replies:

> As rich shall Romeo by his lady lie;
> Poor sacrifices of our enmity!   V. iii

The stress, at the last, is on the value and effectiveness of love's sacrifice: it has ended "the ancient grudge". This is not a mere *coup de théâtre*. Shakespeare has reached his conclusion by measured steps, and by the same gradation we must follow him.

*   *   *

I have already suggested that Coleridge may have been right—if not by argument, then by intuition—in giving Shakespeare the credit for making Romeo love-bewildered at the opening of the play. In establishing his hero's state of mind, Brooke or no Brooke, Shakespeare is conforming with his own method when he makes Romeo exclaim:

> I have lost myself; I am not here;
> This is not Romeo—   I. i

But it is Shakespeare, and at his most deliberate. He regularly shows the development of his characters to be a function of self-knowledge, or of self-discovery. And love and the self, as we have seen, are invariably linked and ultimately united. If Romeo has lost the reality of himself, then he has not found the reality of love. He is in the phase of shadow-worship, and is partly aware of it:

> These happy masks that kiss fair ladies' brows,
> Being black, put us in mind they hide the fair—
>   I. i

It is the familiar theme, "Love doth approach disguised", and there follows a lament for the lack of true love-sight that would pierce the disguise:

> Alas, that love, whose view is muffled still,
> Should without eyes see pathways to his will!
>   I. i

The pity is that they are the wrong pathways. At this phase, as Julia has told us, "Love is a blinded god"; but he receives his sight when the hero, allegorically speaking, recognizes the love-ideal in the heroine:

> Love doth to her eyes repair,
> To help him of his blindness;
> And, being help'd, inhabits there.
>   *T.G.V.* IV. ii

All these principles, which we have found enunciated elsewhere, are reaffirmed in Romeo—who, for the moment, "makes himself an artificial night"—and the only conclusion we can come to is that, whatever use Shakespeare made of Brooke, his own self-consistency is steadfast.

Romeo's love-bewilderment is further emphasized by his speechful of paradoxes, of which *The Romance of the Rose* is the ultimate source[1]:

> Why then, O brawling love! O loving hate!
> O any thing, of nothing first created!
> O heavy lightness! serious vanity!
>
> Misshapen chaos of well-seeming forms!
> Feather of lead, bright smoke, cold fire, sick
>   health!
> Still-waking sleep, that is not what it is!
> This love feel I, that feel no love in this.   I. i

That is the point: true love is not felt in this way. This is only a "fume of sighs", "moonshine in the water".

But Romeo is about to discover reality. As he and his friends stand outside the house of the Capulets, where he will have his first sight of Juliet, Benvolio says to him:

> The date is out of such prolixity;
> We'll have no Cupid hoodwink'd with a scarf—
>   I. iv

They are discussing how they shall present themselves; but the double-meaning, here, is indubitable. The prolixity of paradox is done with. The time of muffled view and artificial night is over. Cupid is no longer to be hood-blind. All the emphasis is now upon clear sight,

---

[1] See above, page 89.

and the dissipation of vain fantasy. And Romeo confirms
it when his eyes fall on Juliet:

> For I ne'er saw true beauty till this night.   I. v

There comes a sound of muted thunder, a warning of
the hate-storm that impends, in the muttered exchanges
between Tybalt and Capulet. Then Tybalt leaves the
hall. And Romeo speaks to Juliet:

> If I profane with my unworthiest hand
> This holy shrine, the gentle sin is this,
> My lips, two blushing pilgrims, ready stand
> To smooth that rough touch with a tender kiss.
> JULIET: Good pilgrim, you do wrong your hand too
> much,
> Which mannerly devotion shows in this;
> For saints have hands that pilgrims' hands do
> touch,
> And palm to palm is holy palmers' kiss.
> ROMEO: Have not saints lips, and holy palmers too?
> JULIET: Ay, pilgrim, lips that they must use in
> prayer.
> ROMEO: O, then, dear saint, let lips do what hands
> do;
> They pray, grant thou, lest faith turn to despair.
> JULIET: Saints do not move, though grant for
> prayers' sake.
> ROMEO: Then move not, while my prayers effect I
> take.
> Thus from my lips, by thine, my sin is purged.
>   I. v

This is a strange first conversation for a boy and a
girl. Certainly, it is not Shakespeare's aim to mirror
nature here. Do romance and poetry explain it fully?
I hardly think so. The religious imagery is too insistent,

too sustained. It suggests allegory. And that, in Shakespeare, means an underlying pattern that will be found elsewhere. Do we find it? The question needs only to be raised to be answered. We first remember that Julia, planning her journey, says she will undertake it as a "true-devoted pilgrim":

> And make a pastime of each weary step,
> Till the last step have brought me to my love;
> And there I'll rest, as after much turmoil,
> A blessed soul doth in Elysium.   *T.G.V.* II. vii

That pilgrimage could be a coincidence, although we are bound to pause over a metaphor so long sustained, and also to remember that the theme of love as religion was emphasized in *Love's Labour's Lost*. But it is Ophelia who dispels all doubt. The creation of Ophelia is nearly ten years later than that of Juliet. So it cannot be coincidental that she holds a key that will turn this lock:

> How should I your true love know
> From another one?
> By his cockle hat and staff
> And his sandal shoon.[1]   *H.* IV. v

We now see that it is nothing less than the distinguishing mark of the true lover that he should be a pilgrim. And Ophelia goes on to characterize in illuminating contrast the false lover, the seducer:

> By Gis and by Saint Charity,
> Alack, and fie for shame!
> Young men will do't, if they come to't;

---

[1] When commenting on these lines in *The Shakespearean Ethic*, p. 141, I had not noticed the theme of love as a pilgrimage in other plays, and my earlier remarks require some modification.

By Cock they are to blame.
Quoth she, before you tumbled me,
You promis'd me to wed:
So would I ha' done, by yonder sun,
An thou hadst not come to my bed.

H. IV. v

There speaks "another one", from whom the true lover
must be distinguished. No explanation of chance or
poetry will account for ten years' consistency. That
love is a pilgrimage to Elysium is a reiterated allegory
in Shakespeare. With due reservations, the same might
be said of Dante, as Snell, writing of the *Vita Nuova*,
has remarked: "the final chapters of the book are
saturated with the twin conceptions of pilgrimage and
vision."[1] Shakespeare was not the first to link together
love, pilgrimage and vision; it is his development of
this association that is original. Despite its joys, the
path of his pilgrims is a rough one. As we have seen
in the case of Julia, and shall see again, love must bear
its cross of sacrifice if it will achieve its crown.

*   *   *

It is important that we should feel quite sure that
Shakespeare is following a love-pattern with full
deliberation, because the allegory is sustained with a
subtlety for which we need to be prepared. After his
first meeting with Juliet, Romeo is more than romantically in love, he is spiritually altered. This is not a
Shakespearean caprice, it has a literary background.
And to this also it is essential that we should give full
weight.

Love/
Religion

[1] Snell, *Handbook to the Works of Dante*, p. 149.

Romeo is now in a state that corresponds, but is not identical with that of Dante at the opening of the *Vita Nuova*. After his first sight of Beatrice, we may remember, Dante begins a new volume in the book of life, headed with a rubric saying, "*Incipit vita nova*". And thenceforward his love-development is traced, in religious language, to its culmination in paradise. The full sweep of Shakespeare's vision is not apparent until we have penetrated his allegories; but when we have done so, we find it is certainly not less than that of Dante. On the contrary, as we may see when we examine *The Phoenix and the Turtle*, the Shakespearean metaphysic is absolute. These are anticipations, and I make them to establish one point: the change in Romeo, although romantically presented, is philosophically conceived; and the birth of the new involves the death of the old. That is the fact which Mercutio is brought on to tell us, "The ape is dead!"

Mercutio, a mere name to Brooke, is all Shakespeare; and we must consider the purpose of his creation. He is dramatically valuable, but dramatic criticism is beyond the field of our enquiry. What is his place in the pattern? Clearly, he is at the mocking stage—that of the "green goose" and the "German clock"—and he does not live long enough to pass beyond it. His astringent wit—compared with the "deal of brine" that Romeo shed for Rosaline—is refreshing; but it is love-blindness none the less. He is in the condition Berowne was in, at the opening of *Love's Labour's Lost*:

—to study where I well may dine,
Or study where to meet some mistress fine—

these desiderata being almost equally appreciated, with the dinner taking slight precedence of the mistress. *Quaerenda est puella* or *nunc bibendum est*—there is little to choose between them. So thinks Mercutio. And not having passed beyond that point himself, he cannot imagine that Romeo is much beyond it either: hence his conjuration of the ape, which fails to raise the familiar in his mistress' circle.

We have already noticed one singularity of Shakespearean construction when we saw how carefully the Launce-and-Crab scenes were set in juxtaposition to those of Julia and Proteus. I think it will be granted that the main reason for this arrangement was not the making of the plot but the presenting of the parable. When once we are alert to the fact that Shakespeare is liable to do this kind of thing, we discover it in other places—here, for instance, in the relation of Mercutio's scenes to those of Romeo. In this relationship, plotting is, of course, important; but allegory was in Shakespeare's mind as well. The Julia-Launce sequence reveals by resemblance: this does so by contrast. It is not merely the contrasting of two men or of two characters, but rather of two stages in the quest for reality.

Reality is an ambiguous word, and for the purposes of studying Shakespeare we must accept his definition. His philosophy, I believe, owes much to Plato. And Plato's famous comparison, in the seventh book of *The Republic*, of the objects that our physical senses perceive to mere shadows on the wall of a cave, is virtually Shakespearean. Throughout the plays, shadow, matter and appearance are contrasted with substance, spirit and reality as the lower world to the higher, earth to heaven. But there is no question, either in Shakespeare or in Plato, of the soul being perpetually chained in the cavern of shadows. At some time, as in a moment of new birth, it will emerge, look upon the world of light, and even make an attempt, which is of small avail, to explain its vision to those who are still immured. This moment of transition from the cave to the light, from the false to the true, is presented in Shakespearean allegory as the moment when the blinded love-god receives his sight.

In both the plays we have discussed, we have seen the importance of this realization. We are about to witness it again. Mercutio's "Adam Cupid" is love in the hoodwinked phase of muffled view, but the word "Adam" remains a puzzle. It might be—though I will not press the suggestion—that there is a play here on the idea of the old Adam and the new, the man of earth and the man of spirit. At all events, Mercutio represents the one, and Romeo has a flash, before the tragedy closes in, of the vision appropriate to the other.

Mercutio makes his first appearance in the scene before Capulet's feast. At the feast, Romeo will receive his love-sight, and behold, as he tells us, "true beauty" for the first time. In contrast to this unveiling of reality, Mercutio delivers a very long speech about Queen Mab. She is our lady of illusion, bringing to everyone some insubstantial dream of his desire. She is the very quintessence of the phase of shadows. And after listening to forty-two lines about her, Romeo, who is so near to bidding her a last good-bye, has had enough:

> Peace, peace, Mercutio, peace!
> Thou talk'st of nothing.   I. iv

Mercutio will not be shut up, but he admits that he is
talking about dreams:

> Which are the children of an idle brain,
> Begot of nothing but vain fantasy,
> Which is as thin of substance as the air,
> And more inconstant than the wind—

There is a little more wind, and then Benvolio brings
the speech to a stop, by making the point to which
Shakespeare has been leading:

> This wind you talk of blows us from ourselves—

Mercutio is silenced, for this scene. He has served his
symbolic purpose. But whichever play we open, we
shall find that, in some form or other, Shakespeare will
face us with this antithesis: the realm of the fairies'
midwife, full of teasing shadows and false shapes, and
the reality that we must discover and be true to in
ourselves. Very soon, Romeo will find his own self in
Juliet's self. And, as Shakespeare makes beautifully
plain, at that level of spirit they are one.

At the feast, Mercutio says nothing. But he comes
into his own immediately after, with his conjuration
speech. This is followed by the balcony scene between
Romeo and Juliet, and the logic of the construction is
now clear. The conjuration speech is to the balcony
scene as the Queen Mab speech is to the feast—a
contrast between two planes of consciousness. But this
time the allegory is more enriched.

The feast is over. We are in a lane by the wall of Capulet's orchard. Romeo enters alone, and halts:

> Turn back, dull earth, and find thy centre out.
> II.i

Then he climbs the wall and disappears. The words simply underline what we have already established— his conversion. Dull earth is to seek, at its centre, the essence of itself. Mercutio and Benvolio now come on; they are looking for Romeo, and Mercutio calls:

> Romeo! humours! madman! passion! lover!
> Appear thou in the likeness of a sigh:
> Speak but one rhyme and I am satisfied;
> Cry but "Ay me!" pronounce but "love" and
>   "dove";
> Speak to my gossip Venus one fair word,
> One nickname for her purblind son and heir,
> Young Adam Cupid—
> He heareth not, he stirreth not, he moveth not;
> The ape is dead— II. i

The Romeo they are looking for, in fact, exists no more. When we see how carefully Shakespeare has built up the allegory to this point, and how meticulously he continues it, we cannot doubt that "the ape" has this double meaning. Nor does he ever cease to regard as a proper study for mankind the antics of the ape-within: we meet the ape, again, in *Measure for Measure*, where the creature, in an angry mood,

> Plays such fantastic tricks before high heaven
> As make the angels weep— II. ii

For Romeo, however, its lamentable love-tricks are now over—in that respect, his ape has had its day. But Mercutio continues in a fine simian style that might move the heavens to laughter. Not finding the body, he proceeds to conjure the spirit of the ape:

> I conjure thee by Rosaline's bright eyes,
> By her high forehead, and her scarlet lip,
> By her fine foot, straight leg, and quivering thigh,
> And the demesnes that there adjacent lie,
> That in thy likeness thou appear to us!　　II. i

Not even a wraith is obedient to this evocation: the one-time magic of its terms is dead. There follow some over-the-port witticisms about "his mistress' circle", and then Benvolio comes back to the theme of love's want of sight. Romeo, he says, has hidden himself among the trees:

> Blind is his love and best befits the dark.

The darkness is Benvolio's own, and it is dwelt on here for the greater glory of the light which will shine in the next scene—*ex tenebris lux*. And for the same constructional reason, the creation of an awakening contrast, Mercutio finishes the picture of what Romeo is supposed to be doing:

> Now will he sit under a medlar-tree,
> And wish his mistress were that kind of fruit
> As maids call medlars when they laugh alone.
> O, Romeo, that she were, O, that she were
> An open et cetera, thou a poperin pear!　　II. i

Witty, smutty—and immeasurably wide of the mark. Romeo is not under a medlar-tree; but in a few moments he will be under Juliet's balcony, and there breathe a wish far from the imaginings of Mercutio:

> O, speak again, bright angel! for thou art
> As glorious to this night, being o'er my head,
> As is a winged messenger of heaven

> Unto the white-upturned wondering eyes
> Of mortals, that fall back to gaze on him
> When he bestrides the lazy-pacing clouds
> And sails upon the bosom of the air.   II. ii

Not even Shakespeare could have contrived antitheses more arresting than the medlar-tree and Juliet's balcony, the poperin pear and love's pilgrim, who has come to the shrine of his own heart's saint—a place so beautiful that we know it must be holy.

There is not a metaphor in the balcony scene that recalls the cave of shadows—unless it is the exhortation to cast off the livery that is "sick and green": everything belongs to a new world of light. The east—the sun—the fairest stars of heaven—the airy region—the bright angel—the winged messenger: not one symbol of dull earth, which before was so insistent, every image is celestial.

If we are to pass beyond this, it can only be into the unity of spirit, or, in Platonic terms, of pure being. Words must falter here, and at last fail utterly. But Shakespeare carries us as far, perhaps, as language will reach in revealing the essence of the self as love. In his philosophy, to realize this and be true to it is to be perfect. It has been said that all art strains towards the free condition of music; and likewise, we may think, all love in Shakespeare, tends towards the union in essence of *The Phoenix and the Turtle*:

> Reason in itself confounded
> Saw division grow together—

And we are brought to the mystical paradox, where not merely language fails us, but conceptual thought. Shakespeare leads his lovers to the threshold of the knowledge of their spiritual identity, which is not, of course, any creation of their own: their love-sight simply shows them that it is.

Ideally, this should culminate in the mystic vision, or philosophic conclusion, of the unity of being, which other explorers—Heraclitus, Plotinus, and many in the Orient—have arrived at by different roads. That Shakespeare chose the path of love must be partly for reasons of temperament, but mainly because the Middle Ages, Neo-Platonism, and the Gospels had prepared his way. I am not, of course, suggesting that Romeo and Juliet here reach this absolute—there would have been no tragedy if they had. I wish to establish a direction. They are moving *towards* what Plato calls "the pure blaze of being", and the Shakespearean path to this is through the "mutual flame".

I have pointed out elsewhere that Shakespeare's heroines lead the hero, if he will follow, to paradise and beyond it, as unerringly as Beatrice guided Dante; but they deliver no lectures; they are unconscious of their role; it is simply their nature, as love-symbols, to be the true beauty and to reveal it. In answer to Romeo's prayer to the "bright angel"—which, of course, she did not hear—Juliet gives him, without knowing that she does so, Shakespeare's pass-key to self-knowledge:

'Tis but thy name that is my enemy;
Thou art thyself—
What's a Montague?
What's in a name?
                         —Romeo, doff thy name,
And for thy name, which is no part of thee,
Take all myself.   II. ii

Love-natural, confines of family
and name

She is speaking simply, out of her heart; but Shakespeare is speaking out of his philosophy. The mask, the favour, the jewel on the sleeve, the portrait—and now, the name. It is one more entry in the long list of disguises:

> Truth may seem, but cannot be;
> Beauty brag, but 'tis not she;
> Truth and beauty buried be.   *P.T.*

Buried at the dull earth's centre. It was to find the centre, the essence of himself, that Romeo came here. And now he is being led towards the discovery that the centre is pure being, the essence love, and that his true self is also hers. This is presented to him as an exchange of selves in the communion of love. And ideally, this should culminate in the consciousness of the divine in all.

Romeo does not achieve this realization. But the ideal standard is in Shakespeare's mind; he is measuring his characters against it: and the degree by which they fall short of it is the measure of their tragedy. Romeo has been described as "Hamlet in love". There are many resemblances between them which it would be confusing to examine here, but one is particularly relevant: each was near to being "man new made", and each of them failed at the last, or nearly the last test. But we must remember that they are being measured against a standard of perfection. In Shakespeare's view, it is not impossible to reach this standard—but it requires perfect constancy to love. And that means to face, in principle, the test of the Cross. If this is passed, there is an out-flow of "power divine", which is a saving grace to a wider sphere; and it is on the assumption that this spiritual power is paramount absolutely that Shakespeare resolves his tragedies. For these reasons, we may rightly speak of the religion of love in Shakespeare: the path goes all the way from the lowest consciousness to the highest; and it is not "the primrose path of dalliance", but the pilgrim's way. In moments of intensity when the parable is receiving special stress, Shakespeare uses religious imagery — sometimes classical, sometimes Christian; it may be Elysium and the oracle of Apollo, it may be heaven and the bright angel, each is holy, each brings the authentic message of the spirit.

So it is here. Romeo, who has been concealed, now steps forward and reveals himself to Juliet:

> Call me but love, and I'll be new baptized—*in Love*
> II. ii

This is one more careful contrast with the preceding scene: the medlar-tree and the balcony, the poperin pear and the pilgrim, and, now, the dead ape and the soul that is new baptized. "Adam Cupid" may or may not be a play on the idea of the old Adam and the new; but the scenes, in the sum of their effects, are set beside each other as earth to spirit. I know that some of my readers will be sceptical of my view of the philosophy implicit here; but I think everyone will grant that Shakespeare is aiming to present more than the romantic exchanges of two young people. At the least, a power is being generated that can, and in the end does, reconcile the Montagues with the Capulets. This love is not a dark-lantern for the lover's use alone:

> My bounty is as boundless as the sea,
> My love as deep; the more I give to thee,
> The more I have, for both are infinite.   II. ii

Shelley made a similar discovery, without any help, I imagine, from Juliet:

> True love in this differs from gold and clay,
> That to divide is not to take away.[1]

Perhaps this is the distinguishing mark of those things that we may rightly call divine—that it is not only more blessed to give them, but more enriching.

*   *   *

For the remainder of the act, Shakespeare follows his source fairly closely, except that he shortens the time. The most important divergence is that he makes Tybalt send a written challenge to Romeo's house. Romeo does not receive it, because he has gone straight from the balcony scene to Friar Laurence's cell. The friar, agreeing to marry the lovers in secret, indicates to us the plot's unfolding scope:

> For this alliance may so happy prove,
> To turn your households' rancour to pure love.
>
> II. iv

This clearly fits Shakespeare's pattern—that the grace of love is a power effective in a widening sphere; but as it is in Brooke, we need not give Shakespeare special credit for it here. The clandestine marriage concludes the act and the protasis of the plot. In the third act, as usual, Black plays its trump card—the killing of Tybalt by Romeo. And although this is also in the source, Shakespeare reshapes the whole episode so characteristically that, for our present purpose, Brooke may be dismissed. The way in which this is handled is

---

[1] *Epipsychidion.*

of great importance, not only to the present play, but to a general understanding of Shakespeare's conception of tragedy and its resolution.

In what may be called the dynamics of Shakespearean tragedy, "the ancient grudge" works like a monstrous pendulum of which the powerful swing does not diminish with the passage of time. It is not difficult to set this going, but it requires a superhuman exertion to bring it to a stop. Lacking this higher intervention, the revenge-sequence will continue in perpetuity, although it is frequently dignified with the names of law and justice. Shakespeare sees no hope whatever in retributive justice and the law that derives from it; and he therefore repudiates the old law in favour of the new. One thing only will bring the tragic pendulum to a standstill—an act of creative mercy. This is not at all the same thing as condoning the offence. It is an outflow of divine power which changes the offender, kills the enmity and leaves the enemy a living friend.

On this principle, as I have tried to show in another place, the Duke of Vienna and Prospero dissolve the evil which would otherwise have turned both *Measure for Measure* and *The Tempest* into tragedies. But spiritual power has to be worked for; and in Shakespeare's philosophy, it can be acquired only through self-knowledge and constancy to love. The hero who can achieve and be true to these will save himself and others; he who cannot, is caught in an *ewige Runde*, on the unmanageable wheel of fate. In later plays, Shakespeare works these things out in detail; but we find a helpful sketch of them in the third act of *Romeo and Juliet*.

163

First, let us watch the perpetual motion of "the ancient grudge". It breaks "to new mutiny" out of precious little. Mercutio and Benvolio are taking a stroll, and Benvolio says:

> I pray thee, good Mercutio, let's retire:
> The day is hot, the Capulets abroad,
> And, if we meet, we shall not scape a brawl;
> For now, these hot days, is the mad blood stirring.
>   III. i

Mercutio, although he denies it, is in the mood to pick a quarrel. Tybalt enters, looking for Romeo, to whom he has sent a challenge, and requests a word with one of them. Mercutio replies:

> And but one word with one of us? couple it with something; make it a word and a blow.
> TYBALT: You shall find me apt enough to that, sir, an you give me the occasion.
> MERCUTIO: Could you not take some occasion without giving?

Benvolio tries to calm them. Then Romeo enters; he has just been married, and Tybalt is Juliet's cousin; but we will consider his intervention on the side of peace, in a moment. Mercutio's reaction to it is:

> Tybalt, you rat-catcher, will you walk?
> TYBALT: What wouldst thou have with me?
> MERCUTIO: Good king of cats, nothing but one of your nine lives—

Swords are out. Tybalt kills Mercutio. Romeo kills Tybalt. There is a tumult. The prince enters, attended by Montague, Capulet, their wives and others. Lady Capulet shrieks:

164

> O, the blood is spill'd
> Of my dear kinsman!—Prince, as thou art true,
> For blood of ours, shed blood of Montague.

So revenge puts on the mask of justice. The manner in which the law of retribution, so far from curing, in fact perpetuates tragedy, is worked out in other plays; but the theme is introduced here, as Lady Capulet continues:

> I beg for justice, which thou, prince, must give;
> Romeo slew Tybalt, Romeo must not live.

The prince replies:

> Romeo slew him, he slew Mercutio;
> Who now the price of his dear blood doth owe?

In this dilemma, Shakespeare's own position is one from which he never shifts a jot in any play: man's guilt is shared by all men; and if strict justice were meted out to everyone, all would be whipped and most beheaded. And therefore, in his view, forgiveness is no foible of fine sentiment: it is an absolute necessity for the continuance of life.

The sentence of the prince on Romeo is banishment. This does not satisfy Lady Capulet. And later, in secret, little knowing that she is speaking of her son-in-law, she says to poor Juliet:

> I'll send to one in Mantua,
> Where that same banish'd runagate doth live,
> Shall give him such an unaccustom'd dram
> That he shall soon keep Tybalt company—
>
> III. v

This is intended as consolation; but in point of fact, she is only making her addition to the forces of death that will destroy her own child. Unwittingly, she is driving Juliet to the scene's last desperate line:

If all else fail, myself have power to die.   III. v

And she is leading herself to the moment of her own agony, when she believes that Juliet has died:

O me, O me! My child, my only life,
Revive, look up, or I will die with thee.
Help, help! call help!   IV. v

Thus Shakespeare shows us the revenge-sequence to be homicidal, fratricidal, and, in the end, suicidal. This is "the ancient grudge" in action, as he sees it throughout his work. In a sense, all who fall as this pendulum of death swings from side to side, are sacrifices. But no healing virtue flows from the victim who dies in hate. He, too, is crucified; but not, as it were, with Christ. On the other hand—and Shakespeare presents this as a universal principle—all sacrifice that springs from love exerts, according to its measure, some power of saving grace. So when Romeo and Juliet die—

Poor sacrifices of our enmity!

—although their sacrifice is far from being perfect, it is effective in its own sphere: the Montagues and the Capulets are reconciled.

*   *   *

Could not the same result have been achieved without the death-ending? The question is to be answered, of course, out of Shakespeare's system of ethics alone: no other standpoint concerns us here. And the reply is,

166

Yes. In later plays where tragedy is resolved—that is to say, in which some chapter of "the ancient grudge" is closed for ever—there is an all-inclusive victory for life. But this depends on the hero's ability to exert, or be a channel for, some more than human power. We see, from the Duke of Vienna and Prospero, that he need not be perfect; but he must be nearly so. Romeo had a glimpse of the world of light, but he was not able to dwell there. He makes an effort to do this, reaches his breaking-point—which Shakespeare emphasizes—and then slips back into the coils of fate. The perfect man, on the other hand, is beyond fate; not in his stars but in himself lies the power that determines his course. He is no longer "Fortune's fool".

When we see that Shakespeare is measuring Romeo, in the third act, by the standard of the perfect man, we understand, first, that his test is a real and decisive one, and, second, that at this stage of his development failure was inevitable. Romeo comes on after Mercutio has begun to pick his quarrel with Tybalt, but before they have crossed swords. Tybalt then turns to Romeo and calls him a villain, to which he replies:

> Tybalt, the reason that I have to love thee
> Doth much excuse the appertaining rage
> To such a greeting: villain am I none;
> Therefore farewell; I see thou know'st me not.
> TYBALT: Boy, this shall not excuse the injuries
> That thou hast done me; therefore turn and draw.
> ROMEO: I do protest I never injured thee,
> But love thee better than thou canst devise,
> Till thou shalt know the reason of my love:
> And so, good Capulet, which name I tender
> As dearly as mine own, be satisfied.

At this, Mercutio breaks in:

> O calm, dishonourable, vile submission!—
> Tybalt, you rat-catcher, will you walk?   III. i

If we place this in a wider context of Shakespearean
ideas, we see that more is involved than the plot of a
particular play. Under great provocation, Romeo is
maintaining constancy to love throughout a sphere of
which Juliet is the centre. The circumference of this
sphere is potentially infinite, although in practice it is
variable. And it is the infinite possibility that gives
spiritual meaning to Shakespeare's heroines as allegorical figures: they are revealers, as Beatrice was to
Dante, of

> *l'Amor che muove il sole e l'altre stelle,*

the love-power that harmonizes all things and brings
cosmos out of chaos. Consequently, when Prospero says
to Ferdinand:

> ———all thy vexations
> Were but my trials of thy love, and thou
> Hast strangely stood the test—   *T.* III. iv

he is stating a principle which enters into all Shakespearean temptation scenes. When the hero fails in
them, he is invariably failing his highest self, which, for
Shakespeare, is the same as failing love; and the consequence is a reversion to chaos, first in his own soul,
and then in the world around him. It is this that gives a
Judas-quality to the tragic heroes, and in some measure
to all men until they are perfect—"man new made".
Romeo, up to the point we have quoted him, has
"strangely stood the test". Like Prospero himself, he

has taken part with his "nobler reason" against fury. It may seem incredible to the audience that Romeo's effort to overcome evil with good would have proved effectual in the given situation; but the impulse of the audience does not constitute a philosophic judgment, and we are bound to infer, from Shakespeare's consistent ethic, that, as love has the power in principle to dissolve hate, it might have done so here. The scale is turned by the fatal intervention of Mercutio.

Twice already we have seen Mercutio made use of not for the plot only, but also for the parable. He was then contrasted with Romeo as love-blindness to love-sight—virtually, as a lower to a higher phase in the unfolding of consciousness. So it is now. To the Mercutio of the conjuration scene, medlars were real, bright angels were not. Here, swords are real, and the power of love is not. To him, the new Romeo is incomprehensible: his vision of Juliet as a messenger from heaven he would have thought ridiculous, and his attitude to Tybalt he finds dishonourable. The under-meaning of Romeo's remark to Tybalt—

I see thou know'st me not—

applies to Mercutio as well; for the outlook of "man new made", which Romeo might have been, is inexplicable to those who do not share it. It was the same in Plato's parable: when a traveller returns to the cave of shadows after a visit to the upper world and attempts to lead the prisoners out, they think him not only mad but wicked, and they put him to death. Invariably, it is from motives of fervent morality that the prophets are stoned. Shakespeare was keenly aware of this; and he exhibits it in later plays as the tragic inversion, in which the hero's false idea of conscience instigates his crime. And it is worth remarking that in his "transvaluation of values", the tragic hero is virtually putting into practice the Nietzschean ethic, which is the diametrical opposite of the Shakespearean. In the present scene, Mercutio believes himself to be acting rightly; but he is the first to draw his sword, and the death-sequence follows.

Romeo's reaction to Mercutio's death seems almost inevitable; and in this, again, he resembles Hamlet. In both heroes, I suggest, Shakespeare is presenting the dilemma of the Christian soul poised—indeed, torn—between the ethic of the Old Testament and that of the New. Both of them, tested to breaking-point, revert to what is, according to the Old Law, justifiable and even obligatory vengeance. By that standard they are not wrong. But none the less, because they adopt it, all hope of achieving the freedom and power of the perfect man is lost, and "black fate" takes over the play. V. S. Pritchett has observed that the ethical demonstration in Shakespeare "becomes important only if we can link the idea of the New Law with the revolutionary person of the new-born man, emerging by something like an ordeal by fire". It may be that Shakespeare had a similar idea. But from the purely dramatic point of view, to fail in the ordeal provides an equal, or even a stronger situation, in which, I suggest, both Romeo and Hamlet are placed. Romeo is, one might say, de-converted. And in his outburst, Shakespeare presents to us, for the first time, his conception of the irrevocable moment in tragedy:

Away to heaven, respective lenity,
And fire-eyed fury be my conduct now!—
Now, Tybalt, take the "villain" back again
That late thou gavest me! for Mercutio's soul
Is but a little way above our heads,
Staying for thine to keep him company:
Either thou, or I, or both, must go with him.

III. i

Black, with these words, plays its winning card of death.
And instantly our thoughts leap forward to the same
horrifying moment in the great plays to come.

HAMLET: —now I could drink hot blood,
And do such bitter business as the day
Would quake to look on.   III. iii

OTHELLO: Arise, black vengeance, from the hollow
    hell!
Yield up, O love! thy crown and hearted throne
To tyrannous hate.   III. iii

ISABELLA: Take my defiance;
Die, perish!   III. i

That is how Black, at the turning-point, plays its hand:
always in the third act, nearly always with the defection
of a major character from the forces of life to the forces
of death. Both philosophically and constructionally
these scenes of spiritual eclipse are of great importance
in Shakespeare. He presents them as a reversion to
barbarism:

        Speak, hands, for me!   III. i

cries Casca, as the conspirators plunge their daggers
into Caesar. Brutus, who loved Caesar, stabs as well.
And after love's grace has been thus forgot, "nothing
goes right". So it is with Romeo. He falls, from near

freedom, back into the vortex of fate. And as he looks at the dead body of Tybalt, Juliet's kinsman, he exclaims:

> O, I am fortune's fool!   III. i

So much is said in this play of fortune, fate and stars —which are nearly synonymous in Shakespeare—that it is necessary to reconsider his views on them. It is plain, from references in several plays, that he is in full agreement with the lines already quoted from Beaumont and Fletcher, and he may have inspired them:

> Man is his own star; and the soul that can
> Render an honest and a perfect man,
> Commands all light, all influence, all fate—

The soul that cannot yet render a perfect man is clearly in a different situation; but it is never completely subject to its fate. If it were, the temptation scenes would have no point. It is a matter of degree; and in the same way that the horizon of the love-consciousness may contract or expand, so do the limits of freedom. The power of the spirit is always paramount in Shakespeare, and freedom varies in proportion as it is exerted. After the killing of Tybalt, when Romeo takes refuge in Friar Laurence's cell, he is in a condition to, "Hang up philosophy!"

> And fall upon the ground—
> Taking the measure of an unmade grave.
>   III. iii

In this state of self-abdication, he is indeed at the mercy of his stars, and little better than a clod of earth. When Shakespeare has made the humiliation of this collapse

painfully plain to us, philosophy is rescued from the
gallows by Friar Laurence:

> Why rail'st thou on thy birth, the heaven and
>   earth?
> Since birth and heaven and earth, all three do
>   meet
> In thee at once—   III. iii

It is clear in Brooke and implicit in Shakespeare that
"birth" here means the time and place of birth—that is,
a nativity in the astrological sense. Scarcely anyone in
the sixteenth century disbelieved in astrology; and
therefore birth, in this passage, is fate. Fate is said to
be conjoined in the soul with "earth" and "heaven";
and we are to assume that the element of earth is
subject to fate, the element of heaven is free from it,
and that man approaches to freedom and perfection to
the extent to which he transmutes the earthly to the
heavenly in himself. The idea is related to the philosophy—of some importance in Shakespeare's day—
that lies behind alchemy, and also to the conception of
the old Adam and the new, the man of earth and the
man of spirit, the one being gradually transformed into
the other.

But the closest parallel to Shakespeare's view that
there is a definite frontier to fate's dominion is to be
found, I think, in a statement made a century earlier by
Pico della Mirandola. In presenting the Neo-Platonic
opinion—by which Shakespeare was certainly influenced—he writes:

> Venus is said to command Fate. The order and
> concatenation of causes and effects in this sensible
> World, called Fate, depends on the order of the

Intelligible World, Providence. Hence Platonists place Providence (the ordering of Ideas) in the first Minde, depending upon God its ultimate end, to which it leads all other things. Thus Venus being the order of those Ideas whereon Fate, the World's order, depends, commands it. Temporal, corporeal things onely are subjected to Fate; the Rational Soul being incorporeal predominates over it; but is subjected to Providence, to serve which is true Liberty. By whom the Will (obeying its Laws) is led to the Acquisition of her desired end. And as often as she endeavours to loose her self from this Servitude, of Free she becomes a Servant and Slave to Fate, of whom before she was the Mistress.[1]

This identification of Venus, Providence and Love—leading to the supreme good—is significant; because we have noticed particularly in Shakespeare that only the soul that yields sovereignty to Love is free and moving towards the climax of life and joy.

* * *

When Romeo learns, from Friar Laurence, that his sentence is banishment, his reaction seems extreme. We feel, as the friar does, that it is overdone, when there is still so much to hope for, to wish that the prince's sentence had been death. Elizabethan audiences had a taste for emotional display, and this may account for it. But it may also be that Shakespeare is inviting us to find something beneath this foaming surface; and if we think back to *The Two Gentlemen of Verona* and recall that Valentine, on hearing of his own banishment, evinced a similar fury of despair, we are obliged to pause. If there is allegory here, it suggests an eviction

[1] Pico della Mirandola, *A Platonick Discourse upon Love* (1487), translated by Thomas Stanley, 1651.

from Eden. It was normal in the Middle Ages to interpret the scriptures allegorically; and Shakespeare may have had this in mind. And he may also have been thinking of the banishment of the lover from the garden of the Rose.

What Valentine, Romeo and the hero of the *Romaunt* are really banished from is, of course, love. In Shakespeare's extended meaning of the word, love and the highest self are one; and the heroine, in her allegorical nature, represents this self-unity. In losing the heroine, the hero is losing contact with, or consciousness of his own higher self, which is clearly a kind of living death. Another glance at Valentine's soliloquy on banishment will make this Shakespearean position plain:

> And why not death rather than living torment?
> To die is to be banish'd from myself;
> And Silvia is myself: a deadly banishment!
> What light is light, if Silvia be not seen?
> What joy is joy, if Silvia be not by?
> Unless it be to think that she is by,
> And feed upon the shadow of perfection.
>
> . . . . .
>
> She is my essence—   *T.G.V.* III. i

I think most people will agree, in view of the persistence of such ideas throughout Shakespeare's work, that this is more than a lament for a lost sweetheart. There are depths of reason below this surface of emotion; and we are intended to take it at two levels—that of a display and that of a philosophy. Surely, only a man with a theory in mind would write such a speech. And as Shakespeare remains constant to the principles of his own system, the illustration is of enduring value.

SHAKESPEARE AND THE ROSE OF LOVE

In *Romeo and Juliet* we have, I believe, the same
psychology, but new metaphors. Juliet is, of course,
love; and she is also presented as heaven. Allegorically
there is no difference; because, as Friar Laurence has
explained, heaven is a content or condition of the soul,
and is realized by love. Severance from the heavenly
element is severance from love, and equally a form of
spiritual death—leaving fate, earth and a torment of
regret. This partial cutting-off of the higher region of
the soul is what Valentine calls "self from self", and is
surely the deeper significance of banishment to Shakespeare. We meet the idea again, and it is something
that is, or seems to be, worse than physical death.
Juliet is speaking by this pattern, as well as from her
own feelings when she says:

> "Romeo is banished": to speak that word,
> Is father, mother, Tybalt, Romeo, Juliet,
> All slain, all dead: "Romeo is banished!"
> There is no end, no limit, measure, bound,
> In that word's death; no words that woe can
> sound.   III. ii

The same terrible stress is laid on it by Romeo himself;
and the briefest summing up of the evidence of our
three witnesses would be that a paradise has been lost.
Romeo's imagery is less subjective than Valentine's,
but the significance of his outburst is the same:

> Ha, banishment! be merciful, say "death";
> For exile hath more terror in his look,
> Much more than death: do not say "banishment".
> .   .   .   .   .
> 'Tis torture, and not mercy: heaven is here,
> Where Juliet lives; and every cat and dog

176

And little mouse, every unworthy thing,
Live here in heaven and may look on her,
But Romeo may not—
                            —"Banished"?
O friar, the damned use that word in hell;
Howling attends it—   III. iii

Like Valentine's and Juliet's, this speech is extreme.
Heaven has been lost. This is partly due to fate, which
has been brooding over the play from the beginning;
the consequence that, in the first act, was "yet hanging
in the stars" is working out. But since the soul, for
Shakespeare, is always more than the toy of Fortune,
there is an element of fault in it as well. Man may do
more than seek for grace, he can create grace by love—
and he must. He can also destroy it:

> Away to heaven, respective lenity,
> And fire-eyed fury be my conduct now!
>   III. i

That is the beginning of Romeo's banishment; and in
the first phase, it is an act of self-banishment. "Self
from self" is in those lines: the heavenly is dismissed,
and the furies are invited. In later plays, Shakespeare
staged this terrible moment, the opening of the soul to
the dark powers, many times, and always with the same
explicit logic.

> Come to my woman's breasts,
> And take my milk for gall—   I. iv

So Lady Macbeth drives out life and invites death. The
divine is disowned, the devilish summoned. For Shake-

speare it becomes almost a ritual act, which Othello and Iago perform upon their knees:

> All my fond love thus do I blow to heaven:
> 'Tis gone.
> Arise, black vengeance, from the hollow hell!
>
> III. iii

This is self-banishment from life itself, and "howling attends it". It is, of course, a matter of degree; but the fact that in Romeo's case it is natural, understandable, and perhaps inevitable, does not make it less real. The alternatives are explicitly stated, and are mutually exclusive. Shakespeare presents to us a universe, not regulated by wavering opinion, but by eternal law; and his work is as faithful a witness to it as is the *Antigone*. Spiritual power is paramount, but it will not be capriciously displayed; its manifestation is equally according to law; and, in Shakespeare's philosophy, it depends on perfect constancy to love. In the last analysis, it is by this ideal standard that his characters are measured; and to the degree in which they fail it, they are self-banished from love and life. That is the allegorical reason for the great stress that, in these two plays, is laid on banishment. In the balcony-scene, Romeo's love-sight gave him a glimpse of paradise. Now it is gone; because, by Shakespeare's reasoning, "fire-eyed fury" is blind to angels, it cannot see the winged messengers of heaven: memory remains, but participation in the fairer world is lost.

Love builds heaven, and hate shatters it. A very similar idea is in Goethe's *Faust*. When Faust has uttered his terrible curse, a lament is heard from the

78

chorus of spirits, "Woe! woe! you have destroyed it, the beautiful world":

> *Weh! weh!*
> *Du hast sie zerstört,*
> *Die schöne Welt—*

But neither for Shakespeare nor for Goethe is paradise irrevocably lost. And the spirits tell Faust to build it again, in his own heart:

> *Baue sie wieder,*
> *In deinem Busen baue sie auf!*

For both poets, this inner reconstruction is always possible. And as Romeo grovels on the ground, "with his own tears made drunk", Friar Laurence points the way to its recovery:

> Go, get thee to thy love, as was decreed,
> Ascend her chamber, hence and comfort her—
> III. iv

The comforting of love is a movement in the right direction, but the full recovery of paradise is not completed in this play. The next scene between Romeo and Juliet is a parting, and they do not meet again on earth. In the balcony-scene, although it took place at night, nearly all the imagery is of dawn and day; now, a heavy stress is laid on night. The waiting Juliet prays:

> Come, night, come, Romeo, come, thou day in
>   night;
> For thou wilt lie upon the wings of night
> Whiter than new snow on a raven's back.
> Come, gentle night, come, loving, black-brow'd
>   night,
> Give me my Romeo— III. ii

179

She has her wish, but for how short a while! In a few hours he will be whispering:

> Look, love, what envious streaks
> Do lace the severing clouds in yonder east:
> Night's candles are burnt out— III. v

* * *

In the fourth act, White—almost always in the form of the allegorical figure of Love—plays its highest card: win or lose, life or death, the game is decided. If the card Black played in the preceding act is unbeatable, Love is shown to us as pathetic, deserted and lost. Such is Ophelia, who is prominent in the fourth act, but helpless: she can only stir our sympathy, which is something; pray for mercy on every soul, which is more, and drown. Lady Macduff, the only good woman in *Macbeth*, is murdered with all her children in the fourth act; it is the martyrdom of love and the slaughter of the innocents; she is doomed and can do no more than suffer. In the fourth act of *Othello*, Emilia and Desdemona do their utmost by protest, appeal and supplication: it is unavailing. On the other hand, when the play is to end with the triumph of life, the action of Love initiates this trend in the fourth act. This is what Mariana does in *Measure for Measure*. Perdita is the incarnation of returning spring in *The Winter's Tale*. And Julia makes love's redeeming sacrifice in *The Two Gentlemen of Verona*.

It is therefore time for Juliet to take action. She goes to Friar Laurence and asks for his advice. With the threat of a forced marriage to Paris now added to her other woes, she is prepared to dare anything:

Or bid me go into a new-made grave
And hide me with a dead man in his shroud;
Things that, to hear them told, have made me
    tremble;
And I will do it without fear or doubt—   IV. i

The friar is not really convinced of her fortitude. He
offers her the desperate remedy of simulated death, but
adds:

If no inconstant toy nor womanish fear
Abate thy valour in the acting it.

Juliet's answer is emphatic:

Give me, give me! O, tell me not of fear!

This plan she follows faithfully—not without terror,
but in spite of it; and the course of the action is now
deflected, and largely determined by her decision.

Why does the plan fail? Why does the death-card
played by Black in the third act win the game? On the
surface, it appears to be due to pure chance: if the
letter Friar Laurence sent to Romeo had been delivered,
the lovers would have escaped together to Mantua, till
the friar found a time:

To blaze your marriage, reconcile your friends,
Beg pardon of the prince, and call thee back
With twenty hundred thousand times more joy
Than thou went'st forth in lamentation—

                     III. iv

This would have been the kind of life-ending that
Shakespeare handles very well in other plays; and if it
does not happen here, it will not be *only* because he is
following Brooke. Shakespeare always adds his philosophic commentary to the stories he borrows, telling

us why, according to his own system of ideas, they turn out as they do. In his view, there are stronger forces than mere chance working against the efforts of Friar Laurence and Juliet for love and life; and this outlook has a bearing on many other plays.

We have traced "the ancient grudge" to the heart-rending line with which Juliet closes the third act:

> If all else fail, myself have power to die.

But death is not the end of it for Shakespeare. He believes in immortality. And many times he makes the point that, in the deeper sense, death solves nothing: the hate-sequence is carried on just as relentlessly both in and from the world beyond. The whole action in *Hamlet* is precipitated by the ghost's demand for retributive justice—and his discarnate will drives the living towards it, corpse by corpse, until his brother-enemy falls in the last blood-soaked scene. Shakespeare's ghosts do more than titillate the audience to agreeable horror; they are psychic forces that may dominate the play; and the crude incident of killing a character on the stage never removes him from the plot. The ghosts throng round Richard on the eve of Bosworth. Banquo's ghost drives Macbeth to what is virtually self-incrimination before his guests. And Brutus tells us exactly how Shakespeare wishes us to envisage the dead men in his plays:

> O Julius Caesar, thou art mighty yet!
> Thy spirit walks abroad, and turns our swords
> In our own proper entrails.   V. iii

These ghosts are neither wraiths nor lookers-on; they are persisting powers, who have lost nothing but their

bodies; and we are intended to sense their participation
in the drama to the last act-drop. They are able to infect
the living with the madness that precedes disaster. And
when Juliet imagines herself regaining consciousness
in the family vault, alone, she says:

> O, if I wake, shall I not be distraught,
> Environed with all these hideous fears?
> And madly play with my forefathers' joints?
> And pluck the mangled Tybalt from his shroud?
> And, in this rage, with some great kinsman's bone,
> As with a club, dash out my desperate brains?
>
> IV. iii

From Juliet's lips, the phrasing is unnatural, and the
concluding action is impossible; but Shakespeare is
making a point of some importance. He sees it as a
general proposition that one consequence of the
perpetuation of hate is that succeeding generations do,
in effect, dash out their own and one another's brains
with their great kinsmen's bones. Nor is that the worst
of it. Although the revengeful dead will lend their bones
for clubs, they have indirect control of more effective
weapons. This brings us to the present instance.
Romeo has already told us that Mercutio—from the
other side of death—claimed Tybalt's life. In the speech
of challenge, in which he dismisses lenity to heaven,
he said:

> —Mercutio's soul
> Is but a little way above our heads,
> Staying for thine to keep him company—
>
> III. i

Mercutio was not kept waiting long. But Tybalt, from
the world beyond, claims a blood-sacrifice as well; and

in view of Shakespeare's way with ghosts, we may take it that Juliet saw one, when she says:

> O, look! methinks I see my cousin's ghost
> Seeking out Romeo, that did spit his body
> Upon a rapier's point:—stay, Tybalt, stay!
>
> IV. iii

Tybalt will not be stayed. He exacts payment to the uttermost farthing, and Romeo meets his own death in Tybalt's tomb. But there the curse is lifted. As Romeo is about to drink the poison, he says:

> Tybalt, liest thou there in thy bloody sheet?
> O, what more favour can I do to thee
> Than with that hand that cut thy youth in twain
> To sunder his that was thine enemy?
> Forgive me, cousin!
>
> V. iii

That half-line, in Shakespeare's scheme of things, changes the tragedy to a spiritual triumph. Romeo pays his debt with constancy to love; and, therefore, there is an outflowing of grace which dissipates the ancient enmity. As he drains the bitter cup, he turns to Juliet:

> Thus with a kiss I die.

And the grudge dies with him. Here is a last and supreme contrast between Mercutio and Romeo. Mercutio died with—"A plague on both your houses!" Romeo dies with a benediction upon both. The one fanned the flames of hate: the other extinguishes them for ever. As we have said, both, in a sense, were sacrifices: and both were effective—in opposite ways. Whatever may be thought of the philosophy it implies, the logic with which Shakespeare presents his revenge-sequence—from the general to the particular, from this life to the next, springing from hell, dissolving in heaven—is so admirably related to his dramatic construction that it has an intellectual beauty of its own. He never lost the conviction on which it rests; and it will be helpful to an understanding of other plays—*Hamlet*, for example—to bear the full sweep of it in mind.

Romeo calls Juliet's tomb "a lantern"—meaning the structure on the summit of a building through which light flows: and from this there would seem to be only one inference that Shakespeare can have intended us to draw—it is in illumination that love's pilgrimage will end. In the course of it, there are inevitable errors. The death of Paris is the last of these. But it is clear that he is included in a reconciliation of souls; and that in a world beyond possessiveness and jealousy, his relation to Juliet—who is a revealer of the true Beauty—will be as perfect as that of Romeo himself. We recall the words of Valentine, "All that was mine in Silvia I give thee." Once again, there is a sharing of perfection. We have entered a sphere where discord is impossible; we have come to Elysium:

> O, here
> Will I set up my everlasting rest,
> And shake the yoke of inauspicious stars
> From this world-wearied flesh.   V. iii

The play ends with one of Shakespeare's most persistent themes: mutual forgiveness is essential. Whatever the past, it has to be accepted, in charity and humility, as a shared fate and a shared fault; on that basis, the future will be better—on any other, it is likely to be worse.

Whenever the Shakespearean hero is offered a choice between love and violence, the one is presented as creative and the other as destructive power. If he reverts to violence, there is a regression towards hell; if he is constant to love, through tests and temptations, there is a dramatic movement towards cosmos and heaven. He is not being measured by our habitual standard; but by one that, in Shakespeare's view, is appropriate to a "perfect man".

Chapter VII

CONCLUSION

OUR enquiry began with a modest aim—to uncover a little of the meaning that the heroine, as a love-symbol, has in Shakespeare. I hope to examine at another time, in connection with Shakespeare's Platonism, the sense in which she is Beauty. That she symbolizes Love—not just romance—was first suggested to me by studying the hero's rejection of her in the tragedies; and I think this view is supported by what we have noticed of the special significance of fourth acts, and of the heroine's activities in them. It would seem that in this, and in several other principles both constructional and philosophic, Shakespeare is consistent throughout his work. And when we examine his background—we might say, his literary foundations —in medieval poetry and thought, we find that there is nothing to surprise us in his use of this and other allegorical figures.

No one doubts the allegory in Spenser. And it is a recognized part of the function of great poets, as everyone would admit with respect to Virgil and Dante, that they should gather up the threads of the centuries, and weave them into a pattern in which the old wisdom shines anew. Considering Shakespeare's pre-eminence as a poet, it would be extraordinary if he failed to do this. And as the allegory of love is by far the most vital and original contribution that the Middle Ages made to poetry and mysticism, we may even wonder, when once we have noticed it in Shakespeare, why we did not expect to find it there. But I think I should make it plain that when I began to enquire into Shakespeare's ethic, I had not the least suspicion of any such thing.

Why is Shakespearean allegory so elusive? Doubtless there are many reasons, but I have already suggested one that seems to me of primary importance. By the orthodox standards of his age, Shakespeare's philosophy was heretical; and having the warning example of the prosecution of Marlowe and others before him, he avoided a similar danger by veiling his ideas. It is not my wish to deny originality to Shakespeare; but he has so much of it that there is no need to impute to him what is not his own, and the ultimate principle of his unorthodoxy is certainly not original. It is one that had been getting the mystics into trouble repeatedly since the early Middle Ages. Shakespeare's view that love leads to the recognition of unity in essence is a poet's presentation of the doctrine of divine immanence. This is something that the mystics are continually re-asserting; and it had been stated concisely by Eckhart, three centuries earlier, in the famous proposition, posthumously condemned, *Ens tantum unum est et Deus est.*

On this mystical foundation, the love-philosophy of the Middle Ages found a perfect support. And we may perhaps see a movement from the principle to an ethic in the saying of a more orthodox mystic, for whom Dante found a place in paradise, Hugo of Saint Victor, "Who would have evidence of God, let him love"— "*Qui vult habere notitiam Dei, amet*".

CONCLUSION

In spite of opposition, when the love "religion" was once established, it survived; and it was fully compatible with the acceptance of Christ as the epiphany of divine love. It is in this form that it appears in Shakespeare. And that is why the judgment and murder of Desdemona, or the trial and condemnation of Hermoine, have, with perfect reverence, a symbolic association with the judgment and crucifixion of Christ, and why all the tragic heroes who betray love have a corresponding link with Judas. But in Shakespearean allegory, these are inner events: the principle of love, and the principle that betrays love are both in the soul. Never to betray, to be constant in service and in sacrifice, is therefore to be perfect.

If, as I think, Shakespeare is consistent, then his whole work must be studied in this connection before reaching definitive conclusions; but even a few plays suggest a philosophic pattern. We are far from understanding it in full—Renaissance Neo-Platonism, which I have omitted from this book, is certainly one of its important elements. But I am not suggesting that Shakespeare's philosophy, even if we were sure of it, is the most important thing about his plays: it is simply one thing about them that we ought to know. Some of his most brilliant critics have doubted or denied that it exists; if they are right, then Shakespeare is unique among great poets in having none. This seems to me improbable, but the challenge of disproving it remains.

Whatever the outcome of the enquiry may be, whether we understand his ideas properly or not, it is indisputable that Shakespeare is still an influence on our thought. Every year, thousands of people see his

189

plays, and hundreds of thousands of words are written about him. There is no other voice from the past to which we still listen so willingly; and this is not merely because he entertains us, even in the highest sense, but also because there is something in his outlook on life that is deeply satisfying. In some way that I will not try to define he is still with us, as Dante, who made the preceding great summation of European thought, has ceased to be.

Great as Dante was, and however much we may admire and love him as a poet and glory in his language, his eschatology is now as alien to us as his cosmogony: both, in fact, await a Copernican revolution. There is nothing to Dante's discredit in this. It was not his mission to escape from the thought of his age, but to represent it. By displaying its scope, he defines its limits. And because of these, Dante's philosophy of love was vitiated by his theology of despair. At the beginning of the *Divine Comedy*, stands the gate of hell. And his hell is not an experience through which many, perhaps all, souls must at sometime pass, but an eternal destination. The inscription on the portals of this vast system of subterranean torture-chambers, bids all who enter to relinquish hope. The mercy of release, and the mercy of extinction will be everlastingly denied to them:

LASCIATE OGNI SPERANZA, VOI CH'ENTRATE.[1]

Within these grim gates, not only sinners are confined, but all the great souls of antiquity. As Virgil, Dante's guide, explains:

[1] *Inferno*, III, 9.

CONCLUSION

"—know, that these of sin
Were blameless; and if aught they merited,
It profits not, since baptism was not theirs,
The portal to thy faith. If they before
The Gospel lived, they served not God aright;
And among such am I. For these defects,
And for no other evil, we are lost;
Only so far afflicted, that we live
Desiring without hope." Sore grief assail'd
My heart at hearing this, for well I knew
Suspended in that Limbo many a soul
Of mighty worth.[1]

Dante does not seem to notice the inconsistency that permits him here, and on other occasions on his journey through the inferno, to feel profound compassion, while the Divine Love itself, of which he speaks elsewhere with incomparable beauty, remains either impotent or unmoved. The system is static. Hell is eternal, heaven is eternal, and between them is an everlasting chasm never to be bridged.

We noticed more than once, in considering *The Romance of the Rose*, how the medieval analysis left us with a pair of unreconciled opposites, and how Shakespeare, whether successfully or not, took up the same problems and tried to construct a synthesis. But there are no extremes in *The Romance of the Rose* so arresting as those of the *Inferno* and the *Paradiso*. And when Dante philosophizes about them, we see that his argument is not really sustained by the reason on which it is supposed to rest. His own vision holds implicitly the synthesis that he did not make. In the last *canto*, he gazes into the divine light—

---

[1] *Ibid.*, IV (Cary's translation).

SHAKESPEARE AND THE ROSE OF LOVE

Nel suo profondo vidi che s'interna
legato con amore in un volume,
cio che per l'universo si squaderna—

Or, as Cary translates the passage:

>   —and, in that depth,
> Saw in one volume clasp'd of love, whate'er
> The universe unfolds; all properties
> Of substance and of accident, beheld,
> Compounded, yet one individual light
> The whole. And of such bond methinks I saw
> The universal form—

In the light of that vision, one might suppose, the
Inferno should have been rewritten. But it could not
have been rewritten by Dante. It was only after the
medieval analysis had been made that a synthesis was
psychologically possible. If I say that Shakespeare
made that synthesis, I realize that many of my readers
will rebel. I will therefore merely give it as my opinion
that he did, and hope that future studies may found the
statement more firmly.

We have, however, come far enough to see why
Shakespeare—or, to put it in general terms, the mind of
the Renaissance—might have made a synthesis, that
Dante—or the medieval mind—could not have made.
It rests on the Renaissance ideal of the "perfect man".
No doubt, this is mainly inspired by the gospel
commandment to be perfect; but it is also related to
the Apollonian, "Know thyself." And even if Ovid's
own thought was as superficial as the context might
suggest, his line, "Only he who knows himself will
love with wisdom", was interpreted by others in depth.

CONCLUSION

These convergent thoughts were bound to lead to an intense preoccupation with the nature of the self. Gifted mystics, of whatever century, may leap to self-knowledge in a moment of insight; but it does not follow that they can tell what they know. It is the poets who must speak. And they cannot proceed *per saltum*. They must gradually build a bridge of symbols that their audience can also cross with understanding, or they will be singing only to themselves.

In the thirteenth and fourteenth centuries, which were notable both for mystics and poets, a marvellous bridge was being built into—and equally, out of—the self. It was constructed by allegory: the method was to personify the psychic contents in order to know them individually, to study the interplay between them, and so to create a language in which the concealed forces that determine action could be discussed. *The Romance of the Rose* is the most important example of this analytical poetry—the most important because it was the most influential, being easily understood and widely read.

The poets of the later Middle Ages, and their audiences, were steeped in *The Romance of the Rose*, and it naturally lead them to the perception of an inner world—sometimes pictured as a kingdom—the perfect ordering of which could bring perfection to the soul. At last, the cryptic words of Christ and Apollo, which only the mystics had been able to fathom in their sessions of silent thought, could be voiced in poetry. From the realization that there was a kingdom within, it was but a step to the assumption that it would become "the kingdom of heaven" if Love were enthroned there.

This was the condition of the "perfect man"; and to discuss the ethics of perfection, in allegorical language, became possible.

But if the inner world could be heaven, it could also be hell. Shakespeare is not a facile optimist. He does not shirk, any more than Dante, the reality of the conditions that make hell. But he differs from Dante in one all-important conception: his hell has no gate. Perhaps he is thinking of Virgil here; perhaps he remembers that it was the doves of Venus that lead Aeneas to the emblem of safe passage through the underworld, the golden bough. But he goes far beyond Virgil. From Shakespeare's hell there is a way to heaven because love is a redeeming principle; and although love may be betrayed, it can never be annihilated—or, if it were, the soul would be annihilated with it, since love, in some measure, is a condition of its existence.

This, I believe, is the Shakespearean synthesis. It is wonderfully expressed in *The Winter's Tale*. It has been suggested before that in *The Winter's Tale* Shakespeare intended to present the whole sweep of the *Divina Commedia* in a single play. If so, then nothing stands out more clearly than the fact that the grim portals of the inferno have disappeared. Hell cannot hold the soul that loves. And it is always possible to learn to love again. But "only he who knows himself will love with wisdom, and according to his powers, perform love's work in full".

> *Qui sibi notus erit, solus sapienter amabit,*
> *Atque opus ad vires exiget omne suas.*

INDEX